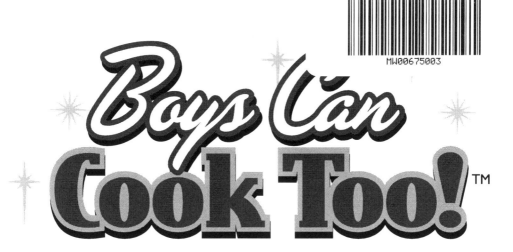

Boys Can Cook Too! ™

An Inspirational Cookbook
for Active Boys of all Ages

Kelly Lambrakis

Throughout this book you'll find this image with a unique 2D barcode inside. Scan the QR code using a smart phone or tablet with a QR reader. You'll be able to access fun and interactive information and entertainment related to cooking. You can download a free QR reader app directly from your phone's app store. As always, ask your parents for permission.

Copyright 2015 Twenty-Three Publishing
Black and White Interior Edition

CookingWithKids4YourHealth.com

ISBN: 978-0-9968131-0-5

Cover Design and Character Illustration
by Laurel Lane

Preface

Boys learning to cook is a vital and healthy part of growing up. I've had my boys in the kitchen since they were toddlers, and put them to work at an early age. I tried to teach them first how to cook their favorite dishes. It's all about getting them involved and letting them experiment. I believe that if they never try, they will never learn how.

In addition to spending time with my boys and doing something I love, it is wonderful to watch them take so much pride in their cooking and manage to have fun in the process.

Kids like to help at a very young age, but then we chase them from the kitchen. We think their "help" will be more work for us, and are also concerned about the dangers. So instead we should take the necessary precautions, teach them the rules of the kitchen, and supervise them constantly. Teaching children from a young age builds confidence. It also encourages them to try new things. Remember, when you finally get young people cooking, do not criticize, or they will lose interest quickly. Teach, show by example, and then let them on their own. In most cases, you will be pleasantly surprised!

Our intention is to have a cookbook that empowers and encourages young adults to build confidence in the kitchen with a life long love of healthy eating.

- Kelly Lambrakis

Hi Boys!

Do you enjoy eating home-made food? Do you wish you knew how to cook, but don't know where to begin?

Many boys think that only girls can cook. Boys Can Cook Too! Did you know that the most famous chefs in the world are men? Men who undoubtedly were active and played sports just like you when they were young.

All the recipes in this book are super kid-friendly, easy to make, and very, very delicious. Every recipe was tested and tasted by active boys just like you. These boys are very active but now they have found room to spend time in the kitchen too.

Boys Can Cook Too! will give you a rookie's understanding of cooking and baking, allowing you to follow and understand recipes with simple, step-by step instructions. Of course, our hope is that this book will inspire you to try more challenging recipes, upping your game and expanding your taste. With lots of practice and many wins (and some losses), you will eventually become an all star chef and more importantly, **"Eat like a Champion!"**

Now, Let the Fun Begin!

Meet our Team of Chefs

Sam

Hobbies: Reading, going to movies with friends, anything with computers

Favorite school subjects: Computers, science

Sports: Hockey, snowboarding, lacrosse, tennis, cross country running

Favorite food to make: Brownies

Favorite Quote: *"You miss 100% of the shots you never take."* – Wayne Gretzky

David

Hobbies: Music, bike riding, fishing, camping and anything outdoors

Favorite school subjects: History, social studies

Sports: Soccer, skateboarding, all water sports

Favorite food to make: Pancakes

Favorite Quote: *"Success is no accident. It is hard work, perseverance, learning, studying, sacrifice, and most of all, love of what you are doing or learning to do."* – Pele

Jake

Hobbies: Going to Major League baseball games, playing video games with friends, drawing

Favorite school subjects: Math, art

Sports: Baseball, football, bowling

Favorite food to make: Pizza, smoothies

Favorite Quote: *"The ball player who loses his head, who can't keep his cool, is worse than no ball player at all."* – Lou Gehrig

Kyle

Hobbies: Collecting baseball cards, hanging out with friends, bike riding

Favorite school subjects: Math, P.E.

Sports: Football, basketball, baseball

Favorite food to make: Mac n' cheese, toffee bars

Favorite Quote: *"Nothing will work unless you do."* – John Wooden

Nick

Hobbies: Playing the guitar, music, writing, acting

Favorite school subjects: English, drama, P.E.

Sports: Basketball, running track, swimming, surfing, golf

Favorite food to make: Cheeseburgers, grilled cheese sandwiches

Favorite Quote: *"Those who work the hardest are the last to surrender."* – Rick Pitino

To Play the Game, You Need to Learn the Rules:

1. Always have an adult nearby to help and supervise.

2. Always wash your hands before you start cooking. Also, wash your hands after handling raw meat.

3. Read the entire recipe before cooking to make sure you have all the necessary ingredients. Also check expiration dates on ingredients that can spoil.

4. Follow the recipes step by step. Missing a step may change your entire recipe.

5. If your recipe calls for fruits or vegetables, remember to always wash them thoroughly before beginning the recipe.

6. When cutting raw meat and poultry, use a cutting board that is used only for meat and poultry. Other utensils and cutting boards should not be touching raw meat and poultry. They should be separate from other foods because they may have germs that can make you sick.

7. Children should not cook anything on the stove, in the oven or microwave without adult help.

8. Always have an adult supervise when turning on appliances, like the stove, oven, blenders and mixers.

9 Always turn off mixers and unplug them when putting in or taking out beaters.

10 Keep all electrical appliances away from water to avoid shock. Never plug in appliances with wet hands.

11 Always ask an adult for help when using sharp knives or utensils.

12 Always turn pot handles on the stove away from yourself.

13 Always use oven mitts when handling hot things. Ask an adult for assistance when taking hot pans in and out of the oven.

14 Always clean counter messes and spills immediately for safety and cleanliness.

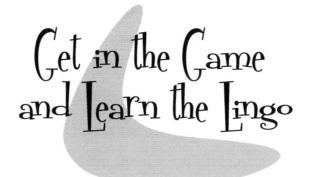

Get in the Game and Learn the Lingo

The following are important terms and techniques you may need to know before you start cooking or baking. If you are unsure of any cooking words, always ask an adult for help.

Al dente – Food such as pasta or vegetables, cooked until tender but still firm, not soft.

Bake – To cook in an oven.

Beat – Mixing ingredients together with a fork, whisk, or mixer.

Boil – To heat liquid to the point that it bubbles vigorously.

Brown – Cooking food until it looks brown on the outside.

Chill – To place food in the refrigerator to make it cool.

Chop – To cut in small pieces on a cutting board.

Cooling Rack – A rectangular metal grid with small holes used to cool hot items on, like cookies.

Cream – To mix butter and sugar together until it becomes creamy.

Cube – To cut food in small square pieces.

Dash – A small amount of an ingredient such as salt and pepper, meaning to shake out in drops from a shaker.

Dice – Cut in cubes of the same small pieces.

Drain – To pour off the liquid through a colander or strainer.

Drizzle – To sprinkle drops of liquid lightly over food.

Fold – To gently combine ingredients together from top to bottom until they are just mixed together, but not over mixed.

Grease – To spread the bottom and sides of a pan with non-stick cooking spray, shortening, butter or margarine. This keeps food from sticking to the pan.

Knead – To mix and work dough, usually with the hands, by folding, pressing, and squeezing.

Mince – To chop very finely.

Mix – To stir ingredients with a spoon.

Saute' – To fry briefly over medium to high heat.

Separating an Egg – Crack the egg on the edge of a bowl, and use your thumbs to gently open the shell in two halves. Pour the egg from one shell half to the other, letting the egg white fall into the bowl, while the yolk stays in the shell.

Simmer – To boil slowly at a low temperature.

Toss – Mixing ingredients by lifting them with a spoon or fork and then letting them drop back in the bowl. You do this when you mix green salad ingredients.

Whisk – To beat ingredients together with a wire whip until well blended.

Scan Me for a fun cooking demo of how to separate an egg!

Equipment

Descriptions of Common
Cooking Utensils and Baking Items

 **Baking Pan** – A square or rectangular pan (glass or metal) used for baking and cooking food in the oven.

 **Baking Sheet** – A flat metal sheet used for baking cookies or other items. Some have 1" sides, also called jelly roll pans.

 **Blender** – An electric appliance used for blending liquids and grinding food.

 Can Opener – A utensil used to open canned foods. Some are electric and some are used by hand.

 **Casserole Dish** – A glass or ceramic dish, usually 1 quart or 2 quart size, used to make casseroles or baked goods in the oven.

 **Colander** – A metal or plastic bowl with holes in it used to drain water or liquid from foods.

 Cookie Cutter – A utensil used to cut dough or pie crust into desired shapes before baking.

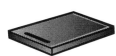

Cutting Board – A board, usually made from wood or hard plastic, used for cutting or chopping ingredients on.

Dry Ingredients Measuring Cups – Cups of different measurements (1 cup, ½ cup, 1/3 cup, and ¼ cup) used to measure dry ingredients, like flour and sugar.

Electric Mixer – An electrical appliance used for mixing ingredients together.

Food Processor – An electrical appliance with a closed container and interchangeable blades that can chop, blend, shred, and puree food at high speed.

Garlic Press – A tool used to crush cloves of garlic.

Grater – A utensil used to grate foods into fine strips or crumbs, like cheese.

Grill Pan – Skillet with ridges that is used to simulate grilling on the stove top.

Ice Cream Scoop – A utensil used to remove ice cream from a carton or other container while forming the ice cream into a ball.

Juicer – A manual or electrical device used for extracting the juice of fruits or vegetables.

 Liquid Measuring Cup – A plastic or glass cup used to measure liquids, with various measurements printed on the side.

 Measuring Spoons – Plastic or metal spoons in different sizes (Tablespoon, teaspoon, ½ teaspoon, and ¼ teaspoon) used to measure either wet or dry ingredients.

 **Muffin Pan** – Metal or glass pan with small or large round cups used for baking muffins and cupcakes.

 **Mixing Bowls** – Bowls in various sizes in which you mix ingredients together.

 Mixing Spoon – A medium or large spoon used for mixing and stirring ingredients.

 Oven Mitts – Mittens or pads used to hold hot pots, pans, baking sheets, and plates. These are sometimes called hot pads or pot holders.

Pastry Brush – A small brush used to spread melted butter, margarine, egg yolk, or sauces over food.

 **Pie Plate** – A baking pan for pie.

 Pizza Cutter – A tool with a rolling cutter used to easily cut pizzas, dough, bread, or tortillas.

 Potato Masher – A tool used to mash cooked potatoes, or anything soft to make them smooth.

 **Rolling Pin** – A utensil consisting of a cylinder (usually of wood) with a handle at each end, used to roll out dough.

 Rubber Spatula – A plastic rubber utensil used to fold foods together or scrape down batter from mixing bowls. Some rubber spatulas are also used for frosting cakes.

 **Saucepan** – A pot with a handle used for stovetop cooking.

 Serrated Knife – A sharp knife used for chopping and cutting firm foods.

Skillet or Frying Pan – A pan used on the stove for cooking food in hot fat or oil. Some skillets are non-stick and can be used for making pancakes.

Spatula – A flat, sometimes metal utensil used to lift and flip foods like pancakes, eggs, hamburgers and cookies.

Toaster – An appliance used for toasting bread.

Tongs – A utensil used to grasp food so it can be moved, flipped, or rotated easily.

Vegetable Peeler – A utensil used to peel the skin off of fruit or vegetables.

Vegetable Scrubber – A brush used to clean vegetables, like potatoes.

Whisk – A utensil used for mixing liquid ingredients, like eggs and milk.

Wooden Spoon – A spoon made out of wood used for mixing and stirring food.

The Scoreboard

Equivalent Measures and Abbreviations

The information below shows measuring equivalents for teaspoons, tablespoons, cups, pints, fluid ounces, and more.

3 teaspoons = 1 tablespoon	2 cups = 1 pint (16 ounces)
4 tablespoons = ¼ cup	4 cups (2 pints) = 1 quart (32 ounces)
5 tablespoons + 1 teaspoon = 1/3 cup	8 cups (4 pints) = ½ gallon (64 ounces)
8 tablespoons = ½ cup	4 quarts = 1 gallon (128 ounces)
12 tablespoons = ¾ cup	16 ounces = 1 pound
16 tablespoons = 1 cup (8 ounces)	Dash or pinch = less than 1/8 teaspoon

**Some of our recipes use abbreviations.
Here are some common ones:**

t = teaspoon	pt. = pint
tsp. = teaspoon	qt. = quart
T= tablespoon	gal. = gallon
Tbs. = tablespoon	lb.= pound
c = cup	# = pound
oz. = ounce	

Temperatures

Fahrenheit	Celcius	Fahrenheit	Celcius
212°	100°	375°	190°
250°	120°	400°	200°
275°	140°	425°	220°
300°	150°	450°	230°
325°	160°	475°	240°
350°	180°	500°	260°

Scan Me for more information about the USDA healthy eating guidelines!

Healthy Eating Pyramid

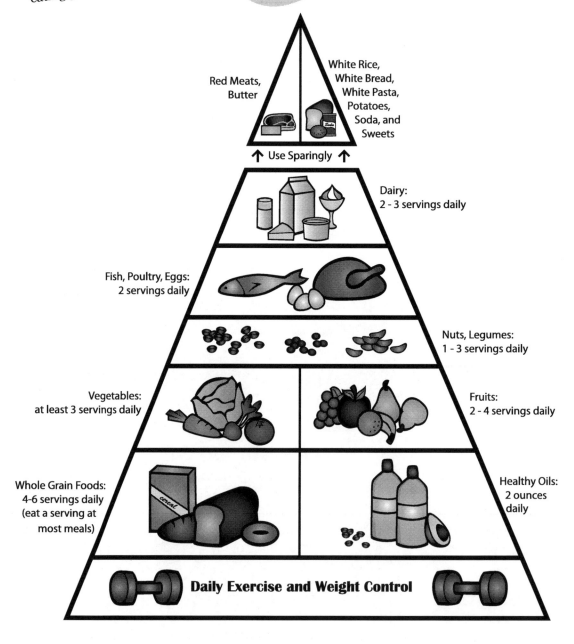

Red Meats, Butter

White Rice, White Bread, White Pasta, Potatoes, Soda, and Sweets

↑ Use Sparingly ↑

Dairy: 2 - 3 servings daily

Fish, Poultry, Eggs: 2 servings daily

Nuts, Legumes: 1 - 3 servings daily

Vegetables: at least 3 servings daily

Fruits: 2 - 4 servings daily

Whole Grain Foods: 4-6 servings daily (eat a serving at most meals)

Healthy Oils: 2 ounces daily

Daily Exercise and Weight Control

Food Groups

The following is a list of wholesome foods that young adults should be encouraged to eat daily. If one learns to enjoy them early, most likely they will be a healthy eater for life.

Whole Grain Bread, Cereal, Rice and Pasta Group - Whole grain foods such as air-popped popcorn, bagels, bran cereals, brown rice, cornbread, whole grain bread, crackers, English muffins, low fat granola, macaroni, oatmeal, spaghetti. The healthy eating pyramid recommends 1 piece or serving of a whole grain food at most meals. The use of white rice, white bread, potatoes, pasta and sweets should be limited.

Vegetable Group - Vegetables such as broccoli, carrots, cauliflower, celery, corn, fresh beans, green bell peppers, peas, potatoes, red bell peppers, spinach, squash, sweet potatoes, tomatoes, zucchini. The healthy eating pyramid recommends at least 6 ounces or 3 servings of vegetables daily.

Fruit Group -Fruits such as apricots, berries, cherries, citrus fruits, dried fruits, kiwis, mangoes, melons, papayas, peaches, pears, pineapples, plums, prunes. The healthy eating pyramid recommends 4 ounces or 2 to 4 servings daily.

Milk, Cheese and Yogurt Group -Dairy foods such as buttermilk, cottage cheese, cream cheese, plain and fruit flavored yogurt, ice milk, milk, ricotta cheese, Parmesan, string cheese and mozzarella. The healthy eating pyramid recommends 2 to 3 servings, with each serving being 8 ounces for non fat and low fat, and 4 ounces for whole fat.

Meat, Poultry, Fish, Dry Beans, Eggs and Nuts Group- Protein such as chicken, extra lean ham, peanuts or reduced fat peanut butter, lean beef, lentils, split peas, beans: pinto, kidney, garbanzo, etc., shrimp, tofu, water-packed tuna, turkey, walnuts. The healthy eating pyramid recommends 1 to 2 servings of poultry, fish and eggs with each serving being 4 ounces. Red meat is suggested to be used sparingly.

Healthy Oils - Plant oils such as olive, canola, soy, corn, sunflower, peanut, and other vegetable oils. The healthy eating pyramid recommends 2 ounces of plant oils daily.

Scan Me for a cooking demo of how to make a healthy breakfast smoothie!

*"Breakfast is my favorite meal of the day. I love whipping up some pancakes in the morning before a big soccer game. **Goal!**"*
— David

Breakfast

Outta the Park Pull Apart Muffins

Prep: 10 minutes
Bake: 10 minutes
Makes: 12 muffins

Ingredients:

¼ cup granulated sugar

1 Tbs. ground cinnamon

½ cup brown sugar

3 Tbs. butter

1 tsp. water

2 cans (7.5 oz. each)
refrigerated biscuit dough

Equipment:

Muffin pan(s)

Small mixing bowl

Measuring cups

Measuring spoons

Paper muffin liners

Mixing spoon

Small saucepan

Oven mitts

*"You owe it to yourself to be the best you can possibly be —
in baseball and in life."*
– Pete Rose

Directions:

1. Preheat the oven to 350°F.

2. Line the muffin cups with paper muffin liners. Set aside.

3. Combine the granulated sugar and the cinnamon in a small bowl.

4. Divide the biscuits and cut each into 4 pieces. Roll the biscuit pieces into balls, and coat evenly with the cinnamon-sugar mixture. Put 6 or 7 pieces in each muffin cup.

5. Combine the brown sugar, butter and water in a small saucepan over medium heat. Bring to a boil, stirring constantly. Allow the mixture to boil until the sugar is completely dissolved, about 2 to 3 minutes.

6. Spoon about a tablespoon of the mixture over the biscuit pieces.

7. Bake for 10 minutes or until light golden brown and the tops spring back when lightly pressed.

8. Using oven mitts, carefully remove the pan from the oven. Let the muffins cool for a few minutes before serving.

Did You Know?

Breakfast is the most important meal of the day. People who eat breakfast in the morning perform better at school and have more energy during the day than people who skip breakfast.

Extra Innings Eggstravaganza

Prep: 10 minutes
Bake: 45 minutes
Makes: 12 servings

Ingredients:

12 large eggs, well beaten

1 Tbs. all-purpose flour

2 cups cheddar/jack cheese, grated

1 package (0.7 oz.) of zesty Italian salad dressing mix

1 container (16 oz.) cottage cheese

1 small onion, minced (optional)*

1 small bell pepper, minced (optional)*

non-stick cooking spray

Equipment:

9 x 13 inch glass baking pan

Medium mixing bowl

Measuring cups

Measuring spoons

Grater

Serrated knife

Mixing spoon

Whisk

Cutting board used for vegetables or fruits

Oven mitts

"In order to excel, you must be completely dedicated to your chosen sport. You must also be prepared to work hard and be willing to accept constructive criticism. Without one-hundred percent dedication, you won't be able to do this."
– Willie Mays

Directions:

1. Preheat oven to 350°F.

2. Prepare the baking pan by spraying the bottom and sides with non-stick cooking spray.

3. In a medium mixing bowl, gently crack the eggs. Using a whisk, beat the eggs thoroughly.

4. Grate the cheese, if needed.

5. Using a serrated knife, mince onions and bell pepper (optional)* on the cutting board.

6. Combine all of the remaining ingredients with egg mixture.

7. Pour the mixture in the glass pan.

8. Bake for 45 minutes or until golden brown on top.

9. Using oven mitts, carefully remove pan from the oven.

10. Let the eggs set for approximately 10 minutes before serving.

Did You Know?

An egg is one of the most nutritious food items in our diet. It is rich in minerals, proteins, and vitamins, all of which are easily absorbed by the body.

Stealin' Home Muffin Sandwiches

Prep: 10 minutes
Bake: 10-12 minutes
Makes: 6 servings

Ingredients:

6 slices of your favorite bread with crusts removed

6 large eggs

¾ cup cheddar cheese, grated

non-stick cooking spray

salt and pepper to taste

Equipment:

Large muffin baking pan

Measuring cups

Grater

Serrated knife

Oven mitts

"Every day is a new opportunity. You can build on yesterday's success or put its failures behind and start over again. That's the way life is, with a new game every day, and that's the way baseball is."
–Bob Feller

Directions:

1 Preheat oven to 400°F.

2 Grate cheese if needed. Set aside.

3 Grease the bottom and sides of a large muffin pan with non-stick cooking spray.

4 Place one piece of bread inside each of the muffin cups, pressing the bottom and sides.

5 Break an egg in each well.

6 Sprinkle with salt and pepper.

7 Top with grated cheese.

8 Bake for 10 to 12 minutes or until golden brown on top.

9 Using oven mitts, carefully remove the pan from the oven. Serve immediately.

Fun Trivia

*Sure, you've heard of hard-boiled, sunny-side, and poached, but have you heard of a **balut** egg? Popular in Southeast Asia, balut eggs are fertilized duck embryos that are eaten right out of the shell. The chick inside is usually not old enough to show its beak, feathers, or claws, and the bones are undeveloped. **I'll take my eggs scrambled, thank you!***

First Down French Toast

Prep: 10 minutes
Bake: 30 minutes
Makes: 6-8 servings

Ingredients:

1 loaf of French bread

4 Tbs. butter

2/3 cup brown sugar

4 large eggs, beaten

2 cups milk

1 Tbs. granulated sugar

2 tsp. ground cinnamon

non-stick cooking spray

Equipment:

9 x 13 inch glass baking pan

Small and medium mixing bowls

Measuring cups

Measuring spoons

Cutting board

Mixing spoon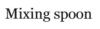

Serrated knife

Wire whisk or fork

Plastic wrap

Oven mitts

"Build up your weaknesses until they become your strong points."
–Knute Rockne

Directions:

1 Preheat oven to 350°F.

2 Prepare the baking pan by spraying the bottom and sides with non-stick cooking spray.

3 In a small (microwave safe) mixing bowl, melt the butter and brown sugar together in the microwave oven for about 30 seconds or until butter is melted.

4 Pour mixture into the pan.

5 Using a cutting board and a serrated knife, carefully slice French bread into 1 inch slices.

6 Lay sliced bread fitting tightly next to each other, on top of butter and brown sugar mixture.

7 In a medium mixing bowl, beat together with a wire whisk or fork, the eggs, milk, sugar and cinnamon.

8 Slowly pour mixture over bread, making sure to soak each piece thoroughly. Spray the top with non-stick cooking spray.

9 Cover with plastic wrap and refrigerate for at least a half hour or overnight, so the egg mixture can absorb in the bread.

10 Remove plastic wrap and bake uncovered for 30 minutes, or until golden brown on top.

11 Using oven mitts, carefully remove the pan from the oven.

12 Serve with butter and maple syrup.

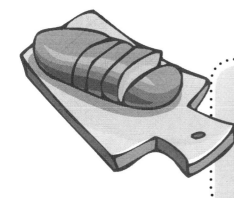

Did You Know?

French toast was created by medieval European cooks who needed to use every bit of food they could find to feed their families. They knew day-old bread could be revived when moistened and heated. They also added eggs for additional moisture and protein.

Bases Loaded Blueberry Muffins

Prep: 10 minutes
Bake: 20 minutes
Makes: 12-14 muffins

Ingredients:

4 Tbs. butter, melted

¾ cup granulated sugar

8 oz. blueberry yogurt or any flavored yogurt

1 large egg

1 tsp. vanilla extract

2 cups all-purpose flour

1 tsp. baking soda

1 tsp. baking powder

¾ cup blueberries, fresh or frozen

Equipment:

Medium microwave safe mixing bowl

Mixing spoon

Measuring cups

Measuring spoons

Muffin pan(s)

Paper muffin liners

Oven mitts

"Only those who dare to fail greatly can ever achieve greatly."
– Unknown

Directions:

1. Preheat oven to 350°F.

2. Prepare muffin pan(s) with paper muffin liners.

3. Melt butter in a microwave safe mixing bowl, about 30 seconds.

4. Carefully remove the bowl from the microwave. Beat in the sugar, yogurt, egg and vanilla extract.

5. Add the flour, baking soda and baking powder, mixing well.

6. Gently stir in the blueberries, until just combined. Do not over mix. Batter will be very thick.

7. Scoop the batter into the prepared muffin pan(s), about ¾ full.

8. Bake for 20 minutes, or until golden brown on top.

9. Using oven mitts, carefully remove pan from the oven.

Did You Know?

Blueberries are one of the only natural foods that are truly blue in color. Blueberries are among the highest antioxidant value fruits that contribute to optimum health and wellness.

David's Out of Bounds Chocolate Chip Pancakes

Prep: 10 minutes
Cook: 5 minutes
Makes: 12 pancakes

Ingredients:

1 large egg

1 cup all-purpose flour
or whole wheat flour

¾ cup low fat milk

1 Tbs. brown sugar

2 Tbs. vegetable oil

1 Tbs. baking powder

½ tsp. salt

½ cup chocolate chips

non-stick cooking spray

Equipment:

Medium mixing bowl

Mixing spoon

Measuring cups

Measuring spoons

Pancake spatula

Non-stick pan
or griddle

"Impossible is not a fact. It's an opinion. Impossible is not a declaration. It's a dare."
– David Beckham

Directions:

1. In a medium mixing bowl, beat together the egg, milk, brown sugar and vegetable oil.

2. Add the flour, baking powder and salt. Beat until smooth.

3. Prepare a non-stick pan or griddle with vegetable cooking spray. Turn the stove on to medium and preheat the pan for about a minute.

4. To check if the pan is ready, sprinkle a few drops of water in the pan. If bubbles jump around, then it is ready to use.

5. Pour about ¼ cup of the batter onto the hot pan. Sprinkle approximately ten chocolate chips evenly onto each pancake. Cook for about 1 to 2 minutes, or until pancakes puff up and are dry around the edges.

6. Flip the pancakes over with a pancake spatula. Cook for about 1 to 2 minutes more, until the pancakes are golden brown.

7. Repeat the steps until all pancakes have been made.

8. Serve pancakes with butter, whipped cream and warm maple syrup.

Did You Know?

The largest pancake in the world was actually cooked in Manchester, which measured 49 feet in diameter, and weighed around 3 tons. Nutritionally, it had a mind boggling 2 million calories!

Scan Me for a cooking
demo of how to make
a healthy chicken
pasta salad!

*"Our football practices are tough, and when it's time for
lunch my friends and I are ready to eat! Getting the guys
together to make our favorite sandwiches is **really cool!**"*
– Kyle

Lunch

Pinch Hitter's Personal Pepperoni Pizzas

Prep: 10 minutes
Bake: 10 minutes
Makes: 12 pizzas

Ingredients:

6 English muffins

1 cup tomato pasta sauce

2 cups mozzarella cheese, grated

24 slices of pepperoni*

Equipment:

Toaster

Serrated knife

Measuring cups

Grater

Baking sheet

Aluminum foil

Oven mitts

"Every great batter works on the theory that the pitcher is more afraid of him that he is of the pitcher."
–Ty Cobb

Directions:

1 Preheat oven to 375°F.

2 Carefully separate English muffins by cutting in half with a serrated knife.

3 Toast all 12 halves of the English muffins in the toaster.

4 Cut in half each of the pepperoni slices. Set aside.

5 Grate cheese if needed. Set aside.

6 Top each half with 1 tablespoon of pasta sauce, then some cheese, then pepperoni, and top with an additional sprinkle of cheese.

7 Place pizzas on a foil lined baking sheet and bake for about 10 minutes, or until cheese is completely melted.

8 Using oven mitts, carefully remove baking sheet from the oven. Serve immediately.

You can substitute the pepperoni for any of your favorite pizza toppings, chopped finely.

Did You Know?

The first pizza was originated in Italy and it was made only of dough and tomato sauce. What? No cheese!

On the Mound Easy Cheesy Mac and Cheese

Prep: 10 minutes
Cook: 10 minutes
Makes: 4 servings

Ingredients:

8 oz. small pasta shells
1 cup whole milk
1 ½ cups sharp cheddar cheese, grated

½ tsp. salt
½ tsp. ground mustard
¼ tsp. ground black pepper

Equipment:

Medium saucepan with lid

Grater

Wooden spoon

Colander

Measuring cups

Measuring spoons

Oven mitts

"The ball player who loses his head, who can't keep his cool, is worse than no ball player at all."
– Lou Gehrig

Directions:

1. Fill a medium saucepan with water until it is about half full. Cover with a lid and heat on medium heat until water boils.

2. Grate cheese if needed. Set aside.

3. When the water starts to boil, add the pasta. Boil uncovered for about 8-10 minutes, stirring occasionally, until pasta is aldente.

4. Drain pasta in a colander. Remember to use oven mitts so you will not burn your hands with the hot water.

5. Put drained pasta back in the saucepan on low heat. Add milk, salt, pepper, and ground mustard.

6. Gradually add grated cheese, stirring constantly, until cheese is melted.

7. Spoon into individual bowls and serve immediately.

Did You Know?

Thomas Jefferson, the third president of the United States, is credited with introducing macaroni to the United States.

Referee's Favorite Pumpkin Chili

Prep: 10 minutes
Cook: 10 minutes
Makes: 8 servings

Ingredients:

2 Tbs. olive oil

1 medium onion, chopped (optional)

2 cups chicken broth or water

1 can (15 oz.) pumpkin puree

2 cans (15 oz. each) kidney beans

1 can (15 oz.) garbanzo beans

1 can (15 oz.) black beans

1 can (15 oz.) tomato sauce

1 packet (1.5 oz.) taco seasoning mix

1 cup cheddar cheese, grated

16 oz. corn chips or tortilla chips

Equipment:

Large saucepan

Grater

Can opener

Colander

Cutting board used for vegetables or fruits

Serrated knife

Wooden spoon

Measuring cups

Measuring spoons

"We are what we repeatedly do. Excellence then, is not an act, but a habit."
– Unknown

Directions:

1. Grate cheese. Set aside.

2. Chop onions, if needed. Set aside.

3. Carefully open beans with a can opener. Using a colander, rinse and drain the beans.

4. Open the pumpkin and the chicken broth with a can opener, if necessary.

5. In a large saucepan, heat the olive oil on low. Add the chopped onions and sauté for a few minutes, until tender.

6. Add the chicken broth or water, pumpkin, beans and tomato sauce to the saucepan.

7. Stir in the taco seasoning. Mix until well blended.

8. Simmer on medium heat for about 10 minutes, or until the chili starts to bubble and heated through.

9. Pour chili into individual soup bowls. Top with grated cheese and corn chips or tortilla chips.

If desired, add a cup of cooked, chopped chicken or turkey to the chili.

Did You Know?

Pumpkins are 90% water, and contain potassium and vitamin A.

Tip Off Tomato Soup

Prep: 5 minutes
Cook: 15 minutes
Makes: 6-8 servings

Ingredients:

4 cups chicken broth or stock
1 can (28 oz.) tomato sauce
1 cup half and half

1 tsp. salt
½ tsp. ground black pepper
mini saltine crackers or
small oyster crackers

Equipment:

Medium saucepan

Can opener

Wooden spoon

Measuring cups

Measuring spoons

"Nothing will work unless you do."
– John Wooden

Directions:

1. Open tomato sauce and chicken broth with a can opener, if needed.

2. Pour the sauce and the chicken broth in a medium saucepan.

3. Heat over medium heat until soup starts to boil, about 5 minutes.

4. Reduce heat to low and stir in half and half.

5. Add salt and pepper. Simmer gently for 15 minutes, stirring occasionally.

6. Serve in soup bowls, garnished with saltine or oyster crackers.

   * Add a couple drops of hot sauce for a spicy kick. Serve with a grilled cheese sandwich for a complete meal.

Fun Trivia

Tomatoes are extremely healthy fruit to eat (yes, tomatoes are actually fruit), but the acid in the juice also has some other great uses. Placing sliced tomato on minor burns will soothe the stinging and prevent blistering. And soaking in a tomato juice bath, will neutralize the nasty smell from a skunk spray. My dog, Maverick, got sprayed on a hike last summer. **It was messy, but it worked!**

Going, Going, Gone Grilled Cheese Sandwich

Ingredients:

2 slices of your favorite bread

1-2 slices of your favorite cheese
(cheddar, provolone, jack)

1 Tbs. cream cheese

1-2 tsp. butter or margarine

non-stick cooking spray

Equipment:

Non-stick pan
or skillet

Pancake spatula

Measuring spoons

Table knife

"It doesn't matter if we're down 3-0. You've just got to keep the faith.
The game is not over until the last out."
– David Ortiz

46

Directions:

1   Spray a non-stick pan or skillet with non-stick cooking spray.

2   Butter one side of the first slice of bread. Place that slice butter face down in the pan.

3   Top with cheese slice(s).

4   Spread the second slice of bread with cream cheese.

5   Place bread, cream cheese side down, on top of the sliced cheese.

6   Butter the top of the second slice of bread.

7   Turn the pan on to medium heat, and grill the sandwich for about 1 to 2 minutes on each side, or until cheese is melted and the bread is golden brown.

Did You Know?

Grilled cheese sandwiches originally showed up in America during the 1920's and was served open face. A grilled cheese sandwich is often accompanied by tomato soup.

Bank Shot BBQ Chicken Quesadillas

Prep: 10 minutes
Cook: 5 minutes
Makes: 4 servings

Ingredients:

½ lb. deli sliced chicken

2 Tbs. chopped onion (optional)

½ packet (.75 oz.) taco seasoning

¼ cup bottled BBQ sauce

4 medium size flour tortillas

1 cup sharp cheddar cheese, grated

salsa

sour cream

non-stick cooking spray

Equipment:

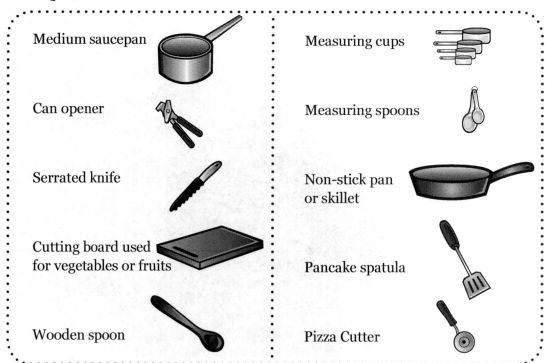

Medium saucepan

Can opener

Serrated knife

Cutting board used for vegetables or fruits

Wooden spoon

Measuring cups

Measuring spoons

Non-stick pan or skillet

Pancake spatula

Pizza Cutter

"Those who work the hardest are the last to surrender."
– Rick Pitino

Directions:

1. Grate cheese if needed. Set aside.

2. Cut deli chicken into bite size pieces.

3. Finely chop onion (optional).

4. In a medium saucepan, combine chicken, onion, taco seasoning, and BBQ sauce.

5. Cook on medium heat until thoroughly heated through and onions are soft.

6. Prepare a large skillet by spraying it with non-stick cooking spray.

7. Put one flour tortilla in the skillet. Sprinkle ¼ cup of the cheese evenly, just to the edge of the flour tortilla. Spoon half of chicken mixture on top. Sprinkle the same amount of cheese over the chicken mixture.

8. Put another tortilla on top of cheese. Spray the top of the quesadilla with cooking spray.

9. Cook over medium heat for 1 to 2 minutes, or when cheese starts to melt and the bottom tortilla is golden brown.

10. Carefully flip quesadilla over, using a spatula. Cook for about 1 to 2 minutes more, or until bottom of tortilla is golden brown, and cheese is melted.

11. Remove tortilla with a spatula and place on a cutting board. Cut in six triangles with a pizza cutter.

12. Repeat steps 6 through 11 to make the second quesadilla.

13. Serve with salsa and sour cream.

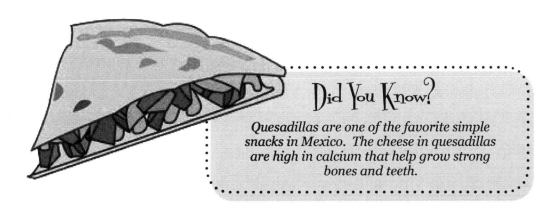

Did You Know?

Quesadillas are one of the favorite simple snacks in Mexico. The cheese in quesadillas are high in calcium that help grow strong bones and teeth.

Time Out Taco Nachos

Prep: 10 minutes
Cook: 10 minutes
Makes: 6 servings

Ingredients:

1 bag (7.5 oz.) tortilla chips

½ lb. lean ground beef

1 packet (1.5 oz.) taco seasoning

1 can (16 oz.) black beans, drained

1 can (11 oz.) condensed cheese soup

1 cup water

1 ½ cups grated cheddar cheese

salsa and sour cream (optional)

Equipment:

Can opener

Colander

Medium non-stick pan or skillet

Grater

Wooden spoon

Measuring cups

Measuring spoons

"Fail to prepare, prepare to fail."
– Roy Keane

Directions:

1. Grate cheese if needed. Set aside.

2. Open the beans and condensed soup with a can opener.

3. Drain the beans in the colander. Rinse well and pour into a small bowl.

4. In a medium non-stick pan or skillet, cook ground beef on medium heat until browned.

5. Using a colander, carefully drain the ground beef.

6. Carefully pour the beef back into the skillet. Add the beans, condensed cheese soup and water. Stir on medium heat, until hot and bubbly, about 5 minutes.

7. Slowly add the grated cheese to the skillet. Stir constantly, until cheese is melted.

8. Serve warm in individual bowls, along side tortilla chips for scooping.

9. You can also serve with salsa and sour cream on the side (optional).

Did You Know?

Nachos were first created in 1943 by Ignacio "Nacho" Anaya. His original nachos consisted of fried tortilla chips covered with melted cheese and jalapeño peppers.

In the Huddle Hearty Beef Dip Sandwiches

Ingredients:

1 pound deli sliced beef, or any leftover sliced beef

2 cups beef broth or stock

1 package (1.5 oz.) brown gravy mix

salt and pepper to taste

4 French bread sandwich rolls

Equipment:

Medium saucepan

Can opener

Measuring cups

Tongs

Wooden spoon

Serrated knife

"The difference between a successful person and others is not a lack of strength, not a lack of knowledge, but rather a lack of will."
– Vince Lombardi

Directions:

1. Open beef stock or broth with a can opener, if needed.

2. In a medium saucepan, combine beef broth with brown gravy mix. Stir until thoroughly combined. Add sliced beef.

3. Cook until heated through and juice starts to thicken, about 5 to 10 minutes. Season with salt and pepper to taste.

4. Carefully cut the French rolls lengthwise, using a serrated knife. Use tongs to fill the rolls with the sliced beef.

5. Serve with individual small bowls of beef juice on the side for dipping.

*Try spreading a thin layer of horseradish on the bread for a little kick. Provolone cheese also goes well on this sandwich.

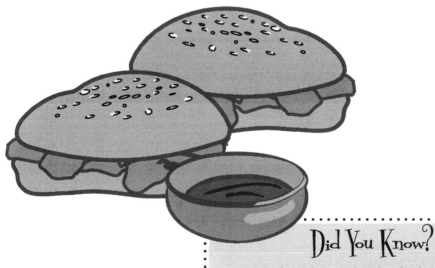

Did You Know?

The beef dip sandwich, also known as a French dip sandwich, was invented in the early 1900's by a chef in Los Angeles who was making a beef sandwich and dropped the French roll into the pan of juices. Customers loved it and the French dip sandwich was invented!

Sam's Breakaway Club Wrap

Prep: 10 minutes
Makes: 1 serving

Ingredients:

whole wheat tortilla, or any favorite tortilla (7" diameter)

2 Tbs. light cream cheese

2 slices deli turkey

2 slices deli ham

1 slice Swiss cheese, or any favorite cheese

1 iceberg lettuce leaf

2 to 3 tomato slices

Equipment:

Serrated knife

Table knife

Cutting board used for vegetables and fruits

Measuring spoons

Paper towel

Plastic wrap (optional)

"You miss 100% of the shots you never take."
– Wayne Gretzky

Directions:

1. On a cutting board used for vegetables, thinly slice tomatoes. Set aside.

2. Wash lettuce leaf with cool water. Pat dry with a paper towel. Set aside.

3. Place tortilla on a flat surface.

4. With a table knife, gently spread cream cheese on one side of the tortilla.

5. Lay the turkey, ham, cheese, lettuce and tomato on top of the cream cheese on the flat tortilla.

6. Bring the sides of the wrap in and then roll up tightly in the shape of a long cylinder.

7. Wrap in plastic wrap until ready to serve.

8. Right before serving, slice wrap in half and remove plastic wrap.

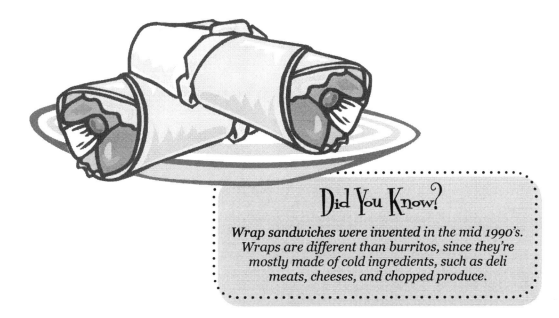

Did You Know?

Wrap sandwiches were invented in the mid 1990's. Wraps are different than burritos, since they're mostly made of cold ingredients, such as deli meats, cheeses, and chopped produce.

Scan Me for a cooking
demo of how to peel
and devein shrimp!

*"After a long day of playing basketball, all I can think of
is hanging out with my buddies and making our favorite
burgers and oven fries. **Now that's a slam dunk!**"*

– Nick

Dinner

Triple Play Honey Grilled Shrimp

Prep:	10 minutes
Refrigerate:	30 minutes
Cook:	4 minutes
Makes:	4 servings

Ingredients:

1 bottle (8 oz.) Italian salad dressing

1 cup honey

½ tsp. garlic powder

2 lbs. uncooked medium shrimp, peeled and deveined

non-stick cooking spray

Equipment:

Small mixing bowl

Mixing spoon

Measuring cups

Measuring spoons

Large zip lock plastic bag

Tongs

Grill pan

8 wooden skewers

"The difference between the impossible and the possible lies in a man's determination."
– Tommy Lasorda

Directions:

1 Fill the baking dish half full with water. Soak the skewers in the water for about a half hour.

2 In a colander, rinse shrimp in cool water. Set aside.

3 In a small bowl, combine the salad dressing, honey and garlic powder. Set aside ½ cup for basting.

4 Pour the remaining marinade into a large zip lock plastic bag, and add the shrimp.

5 Seal the bag and gently turn to coat. Refrigerate for 30 minutes.

6 Drain and discard the marinade. Thread the shrimp onto the skewers.

7 Prepare the grill pan by spraying it with non-stick cooking spray. Preheat the pan on medium heat.

8 Lay 4 skewers at a time across the pan and grill for about 1 to 2 minutes on each side or until the shrimp turns pink, basting frequently with the reserved marinade. Carefully use tongs to turn the skewers over on the grill pan.

9 Repeat steps 7 and 8 until all the shrimp skewers are cooked.

Did You Know?

Shrimp is very high in protein and the high percentage of "good fats" in shrimp reduces the impact of cholesterol in your body. Shrimp also is a very good source of vitamin D and vitamin B12.

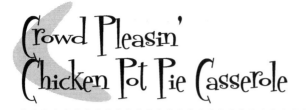

Crowd Pleasin' Chicken Pot Pie Casserole

Prep: 15 minutes
Bake: 45 minutes
Makes: 8 servings

Ingredients:

4 chicken breasts, uncooked, cut in bite size pieces

1 can (11 oz.) cream of chicken soup

1 can (11 oz.) cream of celery soup

1 cup frozen vegetables, (green beans, carrots and corn)

1 cup frozen hash brown potatoes, cubed

1 cup milk

1 cup all-purpose baking mix

½ tsp. salt

½ tsp. pepper

non-stick cooking spray

Equipment:

Cutting board used for poultry

Serrated knife

Large non-stick pan or skillet

Tongs

Large mixing bowl

Mixing spoon

9 x 13 inch glass baking pan

Can opener

"Remember this, the choices you make in life, make you."
– John Wooden

Directions:

1. Preheat oven to 350°F.

2. With a cutting board used only for poultry, cut chicken breasts into bite size pieces.

3. Wash hands with soap and water thoroughly before going to next step.

4. Prepare a large skillet or pan with non-stick cooking spray.

5. Using tongs, add chicken pieces. Sprinkle with salt and pepper.

6. Cook on medium heat, turning occasionally with the tongs, for 10 minutes or until chicken is cooked, and golden brown on both sides.

7. Open soups with can opener.

8. Add the soups to the pan, stirring well.

9. Turn off the heat. Add the vegetables, hash brown potatoes, milk, baking mix, salt and pepper. Mix well.

10. Prepare the bottom and sides of a 9 x 13 inch glass baking pan with non stick cooking spray.

11. Pour mixture in the pan. Bake uncovered for 45 minutes, or until golden brown on top.

Did You Know?

The chicken pot pie was the first frozen pot pie available in the United States, developed by the Swanson company in 1951.

On the Bench Easy Lasagna

Prep: 20 minutes
Bake: 1 hour
Makes: 8-12 servings

Ingredients:

1 pound ground Italian sausage, or lean ground beef, turkey or chicken*

2 cans (15 oz. each) tomato sauce

2 cans (6 oz. each) tomato paste

2 tsp. granulated sugar

1 tsp. garlic powder

1 tsp. Italian seasoning

1 tsp. salt

2 large eggs

3 cups (24 oz.) small curd cottage cheese

1 cup (8 oz.) low fat ricotta cheese

½ cup freshly grated parmesan cheese

1 package (10 oz.) no-boil lasagna noodles

9 slices (4" diameter) provolone cheese

1 ½ cups grated low fat mozzarella cheese

Equipment:

Large saucepan

Wooden spoon

Colander

Measuring cups

Measuring spoons

9 x 13 inch glass baking pan

Grater

Medium mixing bowl

Fork

Mixing spoon

Aluminum foil

Oven mitts

"Everyone has the desire to win, but only champions have the desire to prepare."
– Unknown

Directions:

1   Preheat oven to 350°F. Grate cheese if needed. Set aside.

2   Brown the meat in a large saucepan over medium heat.
Using a colander, drain off excess fat.

3   Carefully return meat to the pan. Add tomato sauce, tomato paste,
sugar, garlic powder, Italian seasoning and salt. Simmer on low
for 10 minutes, stirring occasionally.

4   In a medium mixing bowl, crack eggs and beat well with a fork.
Add cottage cheese, ricotta cheese, parmesan cheese and
1 cup of the mozzarella cheese.

5   Pour about 1 cup of the meat sauce on the bottom of the glass baking pan.

6   Layer uncooked noodles, overlapping slightly on sauce. Layer three slices of the
provolone cheese. Cover with about 1 ½ cups of meat sauce, spreading evenly.

7   Spread half of cheese filling over sauce. Repeat layers of noodles, three slices
of provolone cheese, meat sauce and cheese filling.

8   Top with layer of noodles and then remaining meat sauce. Sprinkle evenly with
remaining three provolone slices and ½ cup of mozzarella cheese.

9   Cover with aluminum foil and bake for 45 minutes.
Uncover and bake 15 to 20 minutes longer.

10   Using oven mitts, carefully remove the lasagna from the oven.
Let the lasagna set for about 10 minutes before serving.

**You may also substitute 2 cups of your
favorite chopped frozen vegetables for
the meat to make a veggie lasagna.*

Fun Trivia

Who said, "When the lasagna content in my blood gets low, I get mean"?
***Garfield the Cat**: This grumpy, lazy, lasagna-addicted Tabby appears in over
2600 newspapers across the world with an estimated 263 million readers
everyday, earning the comic strip a place in the Guinness Book of Records.*
Who knew you could be so famous for what you eat!

Running Back's Greek Supper

Prep: 10 minutes
Cook: 15 minutes
Makes: 4 servings

Ingredients:

½ lb. ground beef

1 small onion, finely chopped (optional)

2 cups beef broth or stock

3 cups (24 oz.) pasta sauce with garlic

½ tsp. salt

1 ½ cups of penne pasta, uncooked

1 cup frozen cut green beans

2 tsp. ground cinnamon

½ cup crumbled feta cheese (optional)

Equipment:

Large non-stick pan or skillet

Cutting board used for vegetables and fruits

Serrated knife

Wooden spoon

Colander

Can opener

Measuring cups

Measuring spoons

"Success isn't permanent and failure isn't fatal."
– Mike Ditka

Directions:

1 Chop onion if needed. Set aside.

2 In a large non-stick pan or skillet, cook beef with onion, over medium-high heat until lightly browned.

3 Remove beef and onions from the skillet. Put in a colander, draining any excess fat.

4 Open the beef broth with a can opener, if needed.

5 Put beef back in skillet and add the salt, cinnamon, broth and pasta sauce. Bring to a boil.

6 Stir in uncooked pasta. Return to a boil and simmer on low heat, covered, about 8 minutes.

7 Stir in green beans.

8 Simmer uncovered for 7 to 10 minutes, until sauce thickens slightly.

9 Sprinkle with feta cheese (optional).

Did You Know?

Pasta (called "zymarika" in Greek) is combined with all types of meats. Greek pasta sauces are known for their wonderful, unique flavor combinations that often include cinnamon and cloves.

Catcher's Favorite Crispy Chicken Tenders

Prep: 15 minutes
Bake: 30-40 minutes
Makes: 4 servings

Ingredients:

12 chicken tenders or 4 chicken breasts cut in thirds (uncooked)

½ cup butter, melted

2 cups corn flakes cereal

½ cup grated parmesan cheese

½ tsp. garlic powder

½ tsp. salt

½ tsp. ground black pepper

non-stick cooking spray

Equipment:

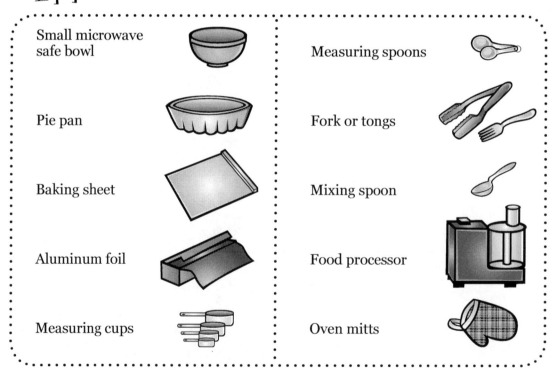

Small microwave safe bowl

Pie pan

Baking sheet

Aluminum foil

Measuring cups

Measuring spoons

Fork or tongs

Mixing spoon

Food processor

Oven mitts

"If you don't know where you're going, you might wind up somewhere else."
– Yogi Berra

Directions:

1. Preheat oven to 375°F.

2. Line a baking sheet with foil and coat evenly with non-stick cooking spray.

3. Melt butter in a microwave safe bowl. Set aside.

4. Put corn flakes in a food processor and pulse for about 30 seconds, or until corn flakes are crumbs.

5. Put parmesan cheese in a pie pan. Stir in the corn flake crumbs, garlic powder, salt and pepper.

6. Wash chicken pieces with cool water. Pat dry with a paper towel.

7. Dip chicken in butter, then roll in parmesan cheese/corn flake mixture.

8. Arrange chicken pieces in rows on the baking sheet.

9. Wash hands thoroughly with soap and warm water before going to the next step.

10. Spray the top of the chicken pieces with non-stick cooking spray oil.

11. Bake chicken for 15-20 minutes, or until one side is golden brown.

12. Using oven mitts, carefully remove baking sheet from the oven.

13. Turn chicken over once, using a fork or tongs.

14. Using oven mitts again, carefully return baking sheet to the oven for a final 15-20 minutes.

15. Remove from the oven when both sides are golden brown and the juices run clear from the chicken.

Fun Trivia

Ever wonder why people call someone a "chicken" to mean they are scared? Chickens are known to be very timid, unintelligent animals that easily freak out. I'd be scared too, if I was going to end up on someone's plate! My parents say sometimes it's smart to be afraid, so maybe I won't mind next time someone calls me a chicken...

What's the Score?... Chicken Tortilla Soup

Prep: 10 minutes
Cook: 10-15 minutes
Makes: 6-8 servings

Ingredients:

4 boneless, skinless chicken breasts cut into 1" pieces, uncooked

1 Tbs. vegetable oil

1 small onion, chopped (optional)

2 cups frozen chopped mixed vegetables (optional)

4 cups chicken stock or broth

1 cup salsa

1 tsp. salt

½ tsp. ground black pepper

tortilla chips

1 cup cheddar cheese, grated

1 avocado, chopped (optional)

Equipment:

Cutting board used for poultry

Cutting board used for vegetables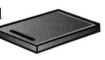

Serrated knife

Can opener

Measuring cups

Measuring spoons

Wooden spoon

Grater

"You can't win unless you learn how to lose."
– Kareem Abdul-Jabbar

Directions:

1. On a cutting board used only for poultry, cut chicken breasts into 1 inch pieces. Set aside.

2. Wash hands with soap and warm water thoroughly before going to the next step.

3. On a vegetable cutting board, finely chop onion (optional).

4. Open chicken broth with a can opener, if necessary.

5. Grate cheese if needed. Set aside.

6. In a large saucepan, heat the vegetable oil over medium heat.

7. Carefully add the cut up chicken, onion and frozen mixed vegetables.

8. Cook for about 10 minutes on medium heat, stirring occasionally.

9. Add the broth, salsa, salt and pepper.

10. Cook until soup is hot and chicken is done. Pour into individual soup bowls, and top with tortilla chips, grated cheese, and chopped avocado (optional).

Did You Know?

Chicken soup of all kinds has acquired the reputation of helping cure the common cold and flu.

Grand Slam Sliders

Prep: 10 minutes
Cook: 10 minutes
Makes: 6 sliders

Ingredients:

1/2 lb. lean ground sirloin beef

¼ cup grated parmesan cheese

1 tsp. garlic powder

salt and pepper to taste

6 small dinner rolls, sliced

6 slices of your favorite cheese

non-stick cooking spray

any of your favorite burger condiments

Equipment:

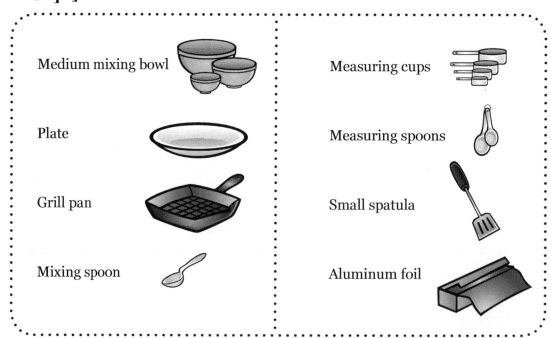

Medium mixing bowl

Plate

Grill pan

Mixing spoon

Measuring cups

Measuring spoons

Small spatula

Aluminum foil

"Baseball is like driving, it's the one who gets home safely that counts."
– Tommy Lasorda

Directions:

1. In a medium mixing bowl, gently combine ground beef, parmesan cheese and garlic powder. Try not to over mix.

2. Using your hands, form the beef to make approximately six ¼" thick patties, a little larger than the size of your dinner rolls. Place on a plate.

3. Wash hands well with soap and warm water before moving to the next step.

4. Prepare the grill pan by spraying the bottom with non-stick cooking spray. Heat the pan to medium. Place the patties in the pan.

5. Wash hands again to remove any bacteria from handling the beef.

6. Season the burgers with salt and pepper.

7. Grill for 2 to 3 minutes or until lightly browned on the bottom side.

8. Carefully flip burgers over with a small spatula. Season with salt and pepper.

9. Grill for a remaining 2 to 3 minutes, or until both sides are browned.

10. Remove burgers from the pan and place on a serving dish. Serve burgers inside sliced small dinner rolls, with sliced cheese and your favorite condiments, such as ketchup, mustard and pickles.

Did You Know?

Mini burgers were nicknamed sliders because they were so small that they'd almost "slide" right down your throat.

Down the Court Chicken and Rice

Prep: 10 minutes
Bake: 40-50 minutes
Makes: 4-6 servings

Ingredients:

6 medium boneless chicken thighs, uncooked

1 ½ cups white or brown rice, uncooked

3 cups chicken broth

3 Tbs. margarine or butter

1 package (1 oz.) dry onion soup mix

1 small onion (optional)

¼ tsp. salt

¼ tsp. ground black pepper

Equipment:

Medium mixing bowl

Large mixing spoon

Measuring cups

Measuring spoons

Can opener

Cutting board used for vegetables

Serrated knife

9 x 13 inch glass baking pan

Aluminum foil

Oven mitts

"If you don't have time to do it right, when will you have time to do it over?"
– John Wooden

Directions:

1. Preheat oven to 350°F.

2. Using a cutting board for vegetables, finely chop onion (optional). Set aside. Open chicken broth with a can opener, if needed.

3. In a microwave safe medium mixing bowl, melt margarine or butter.

4. Remove from the microwave and add the rice, chicken broth, water, onion, salt, pepper, and half of the package of onion soup mix. Mix well.

5. Prepare a 9 x 13 inch glass baking pan, by spraying the bottom and sides with non-stick cooking spray. Pour rice mixture into the baking dish, spreading evenly.

6. Rinse chicken thighs in cool water and pat dry with a paper towel. Sprinkle both sides with salt and pepper.

7. Put chicken on top of the rice mixture in the baking pan. Wash hands thoroughly with soap and warm water before going to the next step.

8. Sprinkle the top of the chicken pieces with the remaining package of onion soup mix.

9. Cover baking pan with foil. Bake for 40 minutes.

10. Remove foil and bake for 5 to 10 minutes longer, or until the liquid is absorbed and juices run clear from the chicken.

11. Using oven mitts, carefully remove pan from the oven.

Did You Know?

More than 90 percent of the world's rice is grown and consumed in Asia, where people typically eat rice two or three times a day. Rice is the staple diet of half the world's population.

Scan Me for
more information
on how to sneak
veggies into
your diet!

*"Hockey is awesome 'cause it's super fast, just like me. I like making side
dishes, like salads, because they're so quick to make and full of vitamins
that keep me energized for my games."*

– Sam

Side Dishes

Overtime Oven Fries

Prep: 10 minutes
Bake: 20 minutes
Makes: 4 servings

Ingredients:

4 russet (baking) potatoes, skin on
3 Tbs. vegetable oil
1 Tbs. olive oil
1 tsp. salt

1 tsp. garlic powder
½ tsp. ground black pepper
¼ cup grated parmesan cheese
non-stick cooking spray

Equipment:

Baking sheet

Aluminum foil

Vegetable scrubber

Measuring cups

Measuring spoons

Cutting board used for vegetables

Serrated knife

Large zip lock bag

Oven mitts

*"Good teams become great ones when the members
trust each other enough to surrender the Me for the We."*
– Phil Jackson

Directions:

1. Preheat oven to 425°F.

2. Spray a foil lined baking sheet with cooking spray.

3. Wash and scrub the potatoes with a vegetable scrubber and cut them lengthwise into 8 wedges.

4. Put potatoes in a large zip lock bag.

5. Drizzle the oil on the potatoes. Add garlic powder, pepper and 2 Tbs. of the parmesan cheese. Close the bag and shake carefully to coat all the wedges with the oil mixture.

6. Spread the potatoes in a single layer on the baking sheet. Sprinkle salt and remaining parmesan cheese on the potatoes. Spray the top of the potatoes with cooking spray.

7. Bake for 20 minutes or until crispy and golden brown.

8. Using oven mitts, carefully remove potatoes from the oven.

Did You Know?

French fries were introduced in the U.S. when Thomas Jefferson served them in the White House during his Presidency of 1801 to 1809.

Goalie's Green Bean Bundles

Prep: 10 minutes
Bake: 30-40 minutes
Makes: 8 servings

Ingredients:

2 cups frozen long green beans, thawed

4 slices of bacon

½ cup margarine

non-stick cooking spray

½ cup brown sugar

1 tsp. soy sauce

1 tsp. garlic powder

salt and pepper

Equipment:

Microwave safe medium mixing bowl

Large mixing spoon

Baking sheet

Aluminum foil

Measuring cups

Measuring spoons

Serrated knife

Oven mitts

*"The highest compliment that you can pay me is to say that
I work hard every day and that I never dog it."*
– Wayne Gretzky

Directions:

1 Preheat oven to 350°F.

2 Melt margarine in a microwave safe bowl. Add brown sugar, soy sauce and garlic powder.

3 Mix together thoroughly, and add the green beans. Toss gently to coat the beans.

4 Line a baking sheet with foil, and spray with non stick cooking spray. Set aside.

5 Cut bacon in half crosswise to make 8 pieces. Divide green beans in 8 bundles, approximately 12 pieces per bundle. Wrap a piece of bacon around each bundle of green beans.

6 Place each bundle on the baking sheet. Sprinkle with salt and pepper to taste.

7 Bake for 30 to 40 minutes or until desired doneness.

8 Using oven mitts, carefully remove the baking sheet from the oven.

Fun Trivia

*Before the next meal, ask your mom or dad for a **plate of Dragon's Tongue**. Do you know what you're asking for? Green beans, of course! Here are a few other strange names for different types of green beans: Burpee's Stringless, Red Swan, Contender, Blue Lake, Cherokee Wax, Pencil Pod Black, Kentucky Wonder, Fortex, Rattlesnake, and Purple King.*

Coach's Favorite Corn Pudding

Prep: 10 minutes
Bake: 40 minutes
Makes: 8 servings

Ingredients:

2 large eggs

1 can (16 oz.) yellow corn, or
2 cups fresh or frozen, thawed

1 can (16 oz.) creamed corn

½ cup butter

1 package (8 ½ oz.)
corn muffin mix

1 cup low fat sour cream

non-stick cooking spray

Equipment:

Microwave safe
medium mixing bowl

Large mixing spoon

Wire whisk or fork

Can opener

Colander

1 quart
casserole dish

Measuring cups

Oven mitts

*"My father gave me the greatest gift anyone could give
another person, he believed in me."*
– Jim Valvano

Directions:

1. Preheat oven to 350°F.

2. In a microwave safe mixing bowl, melt butter in the microwave, approximately 20 seconds.

3. Let butter cool slightly. Add the eggs and beat well with a whisk or fork.

4. Open the cans of corn with a can opener, if needed. Drain the whole corn in a colander if you are not using fresh corn.

5. Add all the corn, muffin mix and the sour cream to the beaten eggs. Mix well.

6. Prepare a 1 quart casserole dish by spraying it with non-stick cooking spray.

7. Pour batter into the casserole dish.

8. Bake uncovered for 40 minutes, or until golden brown on top.

9. Using oven mitts, carefully remove casserole dish from the oven.

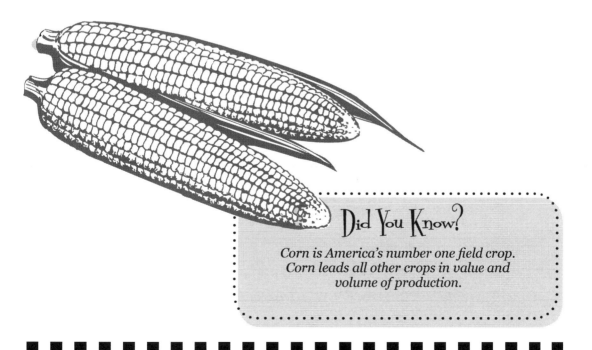

Did You Know?

Corn is America's number one field crop. Corn leads all other crops in value and volume of production.

Double Play Cheesy Potato Bake

Prep: 10 minutes
Bake: 1 hour
Makes: 12 servings

Ingredients:

2 cans (10 ¾ oz. each) cream of chicken soup

1 container (8 oz.) sour cream

2 lb. bag of frozen cubed potato hash browns, about 4 cups

¾ cup grated sharp cheddar cheese

¾ cup grated jack cheese

1 tsp. salt

½ tsp. ground black pepper

4 green onions, sliced (optional)

non-stick cooking spray

Equipment:

Large mixing bowl

Large mixing spoon

Measuring cups

Measuring spoons

Can opener

Cutting board used for vegetables

Serrated knife

Grater

9 x 13 inch glass baking pan

Oven mitts

"Guessing what the pitcher is going to throw is eighty percent of being a successful hitter. The other twenty percent is just execution."
– Hank Aaron

Directions:

1. Preheat oven to 375°F.

2. Open cans of soup with a can opener.

3. In a large mixing bowl, combine soup, sour cream, salt and pepper. Blend well.

4. Grate cheeses, if necessary, and slice onions (optional). Add to mixture.

5. Stir in frozen potatoes.

6. Prepare a 9 x 13 inch glass baking pan by spraying the bottom and sides with cooking spray.

7. Pour mixture into baking dish, and spray cooking spray on top.

8. Bake uncovered for approximately 1 hour or until bubbling and top is golden brown.

9. Using oven mitts, carefully remove pan from the oven.

Did You Know?

Potatoes are definitely America's favorite vegetable. Did you know that every year we consume about 140 pounds of potatoes per person?

On Deck Ranch Salad

Prep: 10 minutes
Bake: 15 minutes
Makes: 6 servings

Ingredients:

8 slices bacon

half baguette sliced into ¾ inch cubes, about 4 cups

2 Tbs. olive oil

¼ tsp. salt

¼ tsp. ground black pepper

1/3 cup buttermilk

3 Tbs. mayonnaise

2 Tbs. apple cider vinegar

1 green onion, trimmed and thinly sliced

1 lb. romaine lettuce, coarsely chopped

1 pint cherry tomatoes, halved

Equipment:

Large salad bowl

Colander

Paper towels

Cutting board used for vegetables

Serrated knife

11" x 17" baking sheet with 1 inch rim

Measuring cups

Measuring spoons

Large mixing spoon

Oven mitts

"Enjoying success requires the ability to adapt. Only by being open to change will you have a true opportunity to get the most from your talent."
– Nolan Ryan

Directions:

1. Preheat oven to 375°F.

2. On a vegetable cutting board, carefully slice the onions. Set aside.

3. Rinse the lettuce leaves in a colander with cool water.
   Pat dry with a paper towel.

4. Tear the lettuce into bite size pieces and place into a large salad bowl.

5. Arrange the bacon in a single layer on half of a rimmed baking sheet.
   On the other side of the baking sheet, add the bread cubes and
   toss with the olive oil.

6. Bake for 15 minutes, tossing the bread cubes half way through.
   The bacon should be crisp and the bread cubes toasted.

7. Carefully remove the baking sheet from the oven. When the bacon
   is cooled, crumble into large pieces with your fingers. Set aside.

8. In a large salad bowl, whisk together the buttermilk, mayonnaise,
   vinegar, salt, pepper and sliced green onions.

9. Add the lettuce, tomatoes, bacon and croutons.
   Toss to coat with the dressing. Serve immediately.

Did You Know?

*Lettuce is a member of the sunflower family.
Americans eat about 30 pounds of lettuce
every year. That's about five times more than
what we ate in the early 1900s.*

Switch Hitter's Broccoli Trees with Cheesy Dipping Sauce

Prep: 10 minutes
Cook: 10 minutes
Makes: 4 servings

Ingredients:

½ lb. of fresh broccoli

1 Tbs. olive oil or butter

1 Tbs. all-purpose flour

¾ cup low fat milk

½ tsp. Dijon mustard

¼ tsp. garlic powder

¼ tsp. salt

¼ tsp. pepper

¾ cup grated reduced fat, sharp cheddar cheese

Equipment:

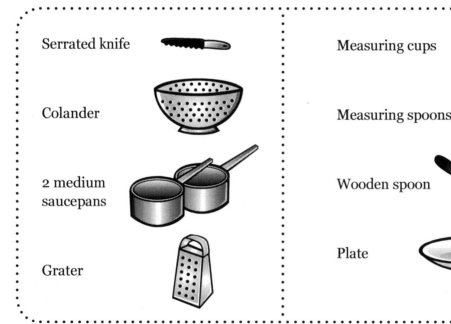

Serrated knife

Colander

2 medium saucepans

Grater

Measuring cups

Measuring spoons

Wooden spoon

Plate

"Risk more than others think is safe. Care more than others think is wise. Dream more than others think is practical. Expect more than others think is possible."
– Unknown

Directions:

1. Grate cheese in a small bowl. Set aside.

2. Cut broccoli in pieces to resemble small trees. Put in a colander and rinse with cool water to clean.

3. Fill a medium saucepan with about ½ inch deep of water.

4. Put broccoli in the saucepan and cover tightly with the lid.

5. Steam on medium heat about 5 minutes, until al dente (cooked until tender, but still firm).

6. Remove broccoli from heat. Drain in the colander and put on a serving plate.

7. In the other medium saucepan, heat oil or butter over low heat.

8. Stir in the flour until it turns golden, about 1 minute.

9. Raise heat to medium. Slowly add milk, mustard, garlic powder, salt and pepper. Bring sauce to a simmer, stirring constantly.

10. Reduce heat and continue to stir until mixture thickens slightly, about 2 minutes.

11. Remove pan from the heat and stir in grated cheese until melted.

12. Serve cheese sauce in four small bowls to use for dipping the broccoli in.

Did You Know?

Broccoli is part of the cabbage family and got its name from the Italian word "brocco" which means branch or arm. Broccoli is high in Vitamin C and soluble fiber.

Drop Kick Cornbread

Ingredients:

2 large eggs, beaten

1 cup cornmeal

1 cup all-purpose flour

1 cup milk

2 tsp. baking powder

¼ cup vegetable oil

1 tsp. salt

1 Tbs. sugar

½ cup corn (fresh, canned, or thawed frozen)

non-stick cooking spray

Equipment:

8" or 9" square glass baking pan

Medium mixing bowl

Measuring cups

Measuring spoons

Wooden spoon

Whisk

Serrated knife

Oven mitts

"Success is no accident. It is hard work, perseverance, learning, studying, sacrifice, and most of all, love of what you are doing or learning to do."
– Pele

Directions:

1. Preheat oven to 400°F.

2. In a medium mixing bowl, combine all the ingredients, except for the corn. Mix well until smooth.

3. Add corn, and gently combine.

4. Prepare the bottom and sides of the baking dish with non-stick cooking spray.

5. Pour the mixture into the baking pan.

6. Bake for 25 to 30 minutes, or until the cornbread is light brown on top.

7. Using oven mitts, carefully remove the bread from the oven.

8. Let the cornbread set for 5 to 10 minutes before cutting.

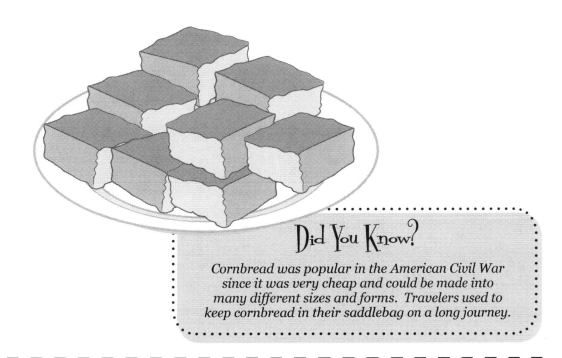

Did You Know?

Cornbread was popular in the American Civil War since it was very cheap and could be made into many different sizes and forms. Travelers used to keep cornbread in their saddlebag on a long journey.

Halfback's Favorite Garlic Cheese Bread

Ingredients:

6 small sourdough bread rolls
½ cup butter, softened
¼ cup mayonnaise

½ cup sharp grated cheddar cheese
¼ cup grated parmesan cheese
2 tsp. garlic powder

Equipment:

Medium mixing bowl

Measuring cups

Measuring spoons

Serrated knife

Table knife

Grater

Baking sheet

Aluminum foil

Mixing spoon

Oven mitts

"Perfection is not attainable, but if we can chase perfection,
we can catch excellence."
– Vince Lombardi

Directions:

1   Preheat oven to 400°F.

2   Grate cheese, if needed.

3   In a medium mixing bowl, combine the butter, mayonnaise, cheeses and garlic powder until spreadable consistency.

4   Slice sourdough bread lengthwise, and spread butter mixture generously on the top of each piece.

5   Prepare a baking sheet by lining the bottom with aluminum foil.

6   Put the bread on the baking sheet and bake for approximately 10 minutes or until bread is golden brown on top.

7   Using oven mitts, carefully remove baking sheet from the oven. Serve immediately.

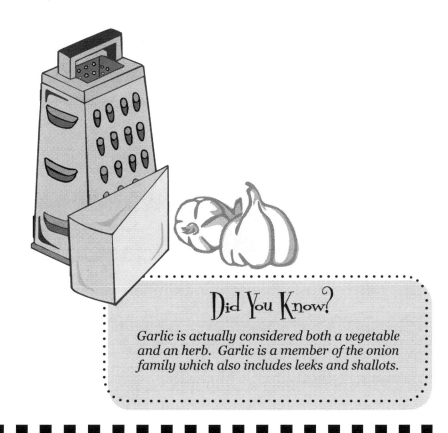

Did You Know?

Garlic is actually considered both a vegetable and an herb. Garlic is a member of the onion family which also includes leeks and shallots.

Scan Me for a cooking demo on how to peel and core an apple!

"Baseball players need to stay in shape. That's why I love these recipes. Not only are they good for you, but they taste awesome and are fun to make too!"

– Jake

Fuel the Body

Healthy Snacks

Center Ice Chocolate Peanut Butter Protein Shake

Ingredients:

2 medium frozen bananas, cut in thirds

1/3 cup peanut butter

2 Tbs. chocolate protein powder (optional)

2 cups low fat milk

2 Tbs. chocolate syrup

Equipment:

Blender

Measuring cups

Table knife

Measuring spoons

"Losers visualize the penalties of failure, but winners visualize the rewards of success."
– Rod Gilbert

Directions:

1. Combine all the ingredients in a blender.

2. Cover the blender with a lid and blend on high speed for about 1 minute or until smooth.

3. Turn off the blender, and then take off lid.

4. Pour into 2 large glasses that have been chilled in the freezer.

5. Serve immediately.

Did You Know?

Drinking protein shakes is a great way to help people achieve their fitness goals. Protein is an important building block in muscle development.

Jake's Home Run Berry Smoothie

Prep: 5 minutes
Makes: 2 servings

Ingredients:

1 medium frozen banana, cut in thirds

1 ½ cups frozen berries of any kind

2 Tbs. vanilla protein powder (optional)

1 cup (8 oz.) vanilla low fat yogurt

½ cup low fat milk

Equipment:

Blender

Table knife

Large mixing spoon

Measuring cups

Measuring spoons

"Baseball is 90% mental, and the other half is physical."
– Yogi Berra

Directions:

1. Combine all ingredients in a blender.

2. Cover blender with a lid and blend on high speed until smooth.

3. Turn off the blender, and then take off the lid.

4. Pour in two large glasses.

5. Serve immediately with straws.

Did You Know?

Berries are loaded with fiber and help you feel full and eat less. Eating one-half to one cup of mixed berries a day improves brain function and physical performance.

Rookie's Favorite Hot Chocolate

Prep: 5 minutes
Cook: 5 minutes
Makes: 2 servings

Ingredients:

3 Tbs. unsweetened cocoa powder
3 Tbs. granulated sugar
2 cups whole milk

½ tsp. vanilla extract
whipped cream (optional)

Equipment:

Medium saucepan

Wooden spoon

Measuring cups

Measuring spoons

"A Winner is someone who recognizes his God-given talents, works his tail off to develop them into skills, and uses these skills to accomplish his goals."
— Larry Bird

Directions:

1. In a medium saucepan, combine unsweetened cocoa powder, sugar and vanilla extract.

2. Heat saucepan on medium heat.

3. Slowly stir in milk to make a paste, then add remaining milk.

4. Cook until thoroughly heated.

5. Pour into mugs and top with whipped cream (optional).

*Try one of the following extra toppings for fun: chocolate shavings, rainbow sprinkles, mini marshmallows, Oreo® crumbles, or cinnamon.

Did You Know?

Chocolate was consumed by the ancient Aztecs as a frothy beverage, somewhat like the hot chocolate we drink today.

Nick's Famous Applesauce

Prep: 10 minutes
Cook: 15-20 minutes
Makes: 4 servings

Ingredients:

4 medium apples

¾ cup water

¼ cup granulated sugar

½ tsp. ground cinnamon

Equipment:

Medium saucepan with lid

Wooden spoon

Vegetable peeler

Cutting board used for vegetables or fruits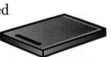

Serrated knife

Measuring cups

Measuring spoons

Fork or potato masher

"Obstacles don't have to stop you. If you run into a wall, don't turn around and give up. Figure out how to climb it, go through it, or work around it."
– Michael Jordan

Directions:

1. Carefully peel apples with a vegetable peeler.

2. Using the cutting board, cut apples into quarters, removing the core with the knife. (You may need an adult to help you with this.) Cut the apples into bite size pieces.

3. In a medium saucepan, combine apples, water, sugar and cinnamon. Cover with a lid, and cook over medium heat for 15 to 20 minutes, or until apples are soft.

4. Remove from heat, and let the apples cool.

5. Gently mash the apple mixture with a fork or potato masher.

6. Serve immediately or you can refrigerate for up to 4 days.

Did You Know?

The first American to orbit the Earth, astronaut John Glenn, carried pureed applesauce in squeezable tubes on his initial space flight.

Tackle Em' Taco Popcorn

Prep: 10 minutes
Bake: 10 minutes
Makes: 2 servings

Ingredients:

1 large bag microwave popcorn, plain

butter flavored non-stick cooking spray

1 tsp. salt

1 tsp. cumin

1 tsp. garlic powder

1 tsp. onion powder

2 tsp. Worcestershire sauce

Equipment:

11" x 17" baking sheet with 1 inch rim

Small and large mixing bowls

Measuring cups

Measuring spoons

Large mixing spoon

Aluminum foil

Oven mitts

"Nobody who ever gave his best regretted it."
– George Halas

Directions:

1. Microwave popcorn according to package directions. Set aside.

2. Preheat oven to 300°F.

3. Put popcorn in a large mixing bowl.

4. Lightly coat popcorn with non-stick cooking spray. Toss and coat again.

5. Combine salt, cumin, garlic powder, and onion powder in a small mixing bowl. Sprinkle over popcorn and toss to coat evenly.

6. Drizzle Worcestershire sauce over popcorn and toss again.

7. Line the baking sheet with aluminum foil.

8. Spread popcorn evenly on the baking sheet.

9. Bake for 10 minutes, tossing once after 5 minutes.

10. Using oven mitts, carefully remove the baking sheet from the oven.

11. Let the popcorn cool before eating.

Did You Know?

Compared to most snack foods, popcorn is low in calories. Oil popped has 55 calories per cup, and air-popped only has 31 calories per cup.

Slam Dunk Caramel Dip and Apples

Prep: 5 minutes
Cook: 5 minutes
Makes: 1 ½ cups

Ingredients:

1 bag (12 oz.) caramels, unwrapped

1 can (14 oz.) sweetened condensed milk

½ cup butter

3 to 4 sliced apples for dipping

Equipment:

Medium microwave safe mixing bowl

Measuring cups

Can opener

Large mixing spoon

Oven mitts

"There is no limit to what can be accomplished when no one cares who gets the credit."
– John Wooden

104

Directions:

1. Using a can opener, carefully open the sweetened condensed milk.

2. In a medium, microwave safe mixing bowl, combine the caramels, sweetened condensed milk and the butter.

3. Microwave on high for 2 or 3 minutes, stirring after each minute or until caramels are melted and the ingredients are blended.

4. Using oven mitts, carefully remove the bowl from the microwave.

5. Serve with sliced apples for dipping. Dip stays soft all day.

Fun Trivia

Fresh apples float because 25% of their volume is air, which makes them lighter than water. That's why apples are great for the fun Halloween game - bobbing for apples. According to the Guinness Book of World Records, the most people apple bobbing at one time was 266. That's a lot of germs floating around. **Yuck!** *Luckily apples are also know as "nature's toothbrush".*

Two Point Fruit Kabobs and Dip

Prep: 10 minutes
Makes: 2 ½ cups

Ingredients:

2 cups part-skim ricotta cheese

½ cup low fat plain yogurt

1 package (5 oz.)
instant vanilla pudding mix

any fresh fruit:
    apples, strawberries,
    grapes, pineapple,
    bananas

Equipment:

Electric mixer

Medium mixing bowl

Measuring cups

Measuring spoons

Serrated knife

Small cutting board used for fruits and vegetables

Wooden skewers (optional)

*"If what you have done yesterday still looks big to you,
you haven't done much today."*
– Mike Krzyzewski

Directions:

1 Using an electric mixer on medium speed, beat ricotta cheese, yogurt and pudding mix together until smooth, about a minute.

2 Prepare the fruit by washing them all, and cutting into small squares. If using bananas, peel and cut in chunks. Cut the pineapple in chunks, if it's fresh.

3 If using skewers, slide pieces of fruit onto the skewer and design your own kabob by putting as much or as little of whatever fruit you want. Do this until the stick is almost covered from end to end.

4 Serve fruit with dip.

Did You Know?

Ricotta is an Italian cheese that is typically made from a mixture of whey and milk and is an excellent source of calcium.

Double Dribble Dessert Nachos

Prep: 10 minutes
Bake: 10-12 minutes
Makes: 4-6 servings

Ingredients:

3 six-inch flour tortillas
(whole wheat or regular)

1 ½ Tbs. granulated sugar

2 ½ cups fresh strawberries,
cleaned and hulled

½ cup shredded coconut or white
chocolate shavings

1 Tbs. orange juice

1 cup (8 oz.) vanilla yogurt

non-stick cooking spray

Equipment:

Blender

Mixing spoon

Table knife

Serrated knife

Cutting board used
for fruits or vegetables

Measuring cups

Measuring spoons

Baking sheet

Aluminum foil

Oven mitts

*"There are only two options regarding commitment; you're either in
or you're out. There's no such thing as life in-between."*
– Pat Riley

Directions:

1. Preheat the oven to 350°F.

2. Prepare a baking sheet by lining it with foil, and spraying it generously with cooking spray.

3. Cut the tortillas into triangles, lay them on the baking sheet, and spray them with cooking spray.

4. Sprinkle 1 tablespoon of the sugar over the top of the tortillas and bake for 12 minutes, or until crispy and lightly browned.

5. Using oven mitts, carefully remove the baking sheet from the oven. Let the chips cool.

6. For the homemade strawberry sauce, combine 1 ½ cup of the strawberries, orange juice, and the remaining ½ tablespoon sugar in a blender. Puree the ingredients until smooth.

7. Chop the remaining cup of strawberries into bite size pieces. Put in a small serving bowl and set aside.

8. Once the chips have cooled, arrange them on a plate.

9. Set out separate bowls with the strawberry sauce, yogurt, chopped strawberries, and coconut or chocolate shavings for serving with the homemade tortilla triangles.

Did You Know?

Strawberries are high in vitamin C, and is the only fruit with edible seeds on the outside. The average strawberry has 200 seeds.

Scan Me for a fun
cooking demo on
how to make easy
banana ice-cream!

*"There's nothing better than celebrating
a victory with a bunch of friends and making
awesome treats to share!"*

Let's Celebrate!

Sweets and Treats

Off Sides Ice Cream in a Can

Prep: 10-15 minutes
Makes: 4 servings

Ingredients:

1 pint half and half cream, very cold

2 tsp. vanilla extract

½ cup granulated sugar

½ cup rock salt

ice cubes

Any one of your favorite add ins:

3 Tbs. of your favorite flavor of instant pudding,

or 1/3 cup chopped fruit such as strawberries, peaches, bananas,

or 3 of your favorite cookies, crushed in small pieces

Equipment:

1 lb. and 3 lb. coffee cans with lids

Mixing spoon

Measuring cups

Measuring spoons

"Life is ten percent what happens to you and ninety percent how you respond to it."
– Lou Holtz

Directions:

1   Thoroughly clean and dry the coffee cans.

2   In the 1 pound coffee can, combine the half and half, vanilla extract and sugar. Add any of your favorite add ins.

3   Place the lid on securely and set it inside the three pound can.

4   In between the cans, surround it with crushed ice and rock salt, alternating layers of ice and salt. When totally full, secure the lid on the large can. You may want to use a heavy duty tape to make sure that the lid doesn't come off.

5   Now here comes the fun part.... Sit on the ground and roll the can back and forth 3 to 4 feet apart. Roll for about 10 minutes. You can also kick the can back and forth as well.

6   Check to see if the ice cream is hard. If it isn't ready, replace the lid and add more ice and rock salt. Roll for another 5 to 10 minutes.

7   Remove the lid to the 1 pound can. Serve ice cream in bowls.

Did You Know?

The ice cream cone's invention is linked to the 1904 World's Fair in St. Louis. An ice cream vendor reportedly didn't have enough dishes to keep up with the demand, so he teamed up with a waffle vendor who rolled his waffles into cones!

Pop Fly Peach Crisp

Prep: 10 minutes
Bake: 30 minutes
Makes: 6 servings

Ingredients:

2 cans (15 oz. each) sliced peaches in its own juice

1 tsp. ground cinnamon and 1 tsp. sugar, combined

¼ cup butter or margarine

¾ cup quick cooking rolled oats

¼ cup brown sugar

½ cup all-purpose flour

2 tsp. ground cinnamon

non-stick cooking spray

Equipment:

Medium mixing bowl

Large mixing spoon

Measuring cups

Measuring spoons

Can opener

8" or 9" glass baking pan

Oven mitts

"It's hard to beat a person who never gives up."
– Babe Ruth

Directions:

1. Preheat oven to 350°F.

2. Prepare the baking pan by spraying the bottom and sides with cooking spray.

3. Open sliced peaches with a can opener, and pour peaches (including juices) in the baking dish, spreading evenly.

4. Sprinkle 1 tsp. cinnamon and 1 tsp. sugar mixture on top of peaches.

5. In a medium size microwave safe mixing bowl, melt butter or margarine in the microwave.

6. Carefully remove the bowl from the microwave and add the oats, ¼ cup sugar, brown sugar, flour and 2 tsp. cinnamon. Mix well.

7. Sprinkle crumbled oat mixture over peaches.

8. Spray top with cooking spray.

9. Bake for 30 minutes, or until golden and bubbly around the edges.

10. Using oven mitts, carefully remove baking pan from the oven.

11. Serve warm with vanilla ice cream.

Did You Know?

The British version of a crisp is called a crumble. The early American settlers had to improvise when ingredients were not available. Colonists were known to serve peach crisp for a variety of meals and often breakfast. By the late 1800's the peach crisp became primarily a dessert.

Rebound Mini Strawberry Jam Pies

Prep: 10 minutes
Bake: 20 minutes
Makes: 12 pies

Ingredients:

2 pieces (9" round) of refrigerator pie crust dough

½ cup strawberry jam or preserves

1 large egg

¼ cup granulated sugar

non-stick cooking spray

Equipment:

Baking sheet

Aluminum foil

3" round cookie cutter or a cup with a 3" circumference

Measuring cups

Measuring spoons

Small spoon

Large cutting board

Fork

Pastry brush

Oven mitts

"One man can be a crucial ingredient on a team,
but one man cannot make a team."
– Kareem Abdul-Jabbar

Directions:

1. Preheat oven to 350°F.

2. Line a baking sheet with foil, and spray with non-stick cooking spray.

3. Open the pie crust dough and lay open on a large cutting board.

4. Using the cookie cutter or cup, cut the dough in approximately 12 circles.

5. Place the dough circles on the baking sheet.

6. Put a rounded teaspoon of strawberry jam or preserves on each circle.

7. Fold each circle over and pinch dough gently with a fork around edges to seal. Turn pie over and seal the other side the same.

8. Poke a few air holes in the pies with the tines of the fork.

9. In a separate bowl, carefully separate the egg, using only the yolk.

10. Beat the yolk with a fork. Using a pastry brush, brush yolk on each pie.

11. Sprinkle each pie with ½ tsp. of sugar. Bake for 20 minutes, or until golden brown.

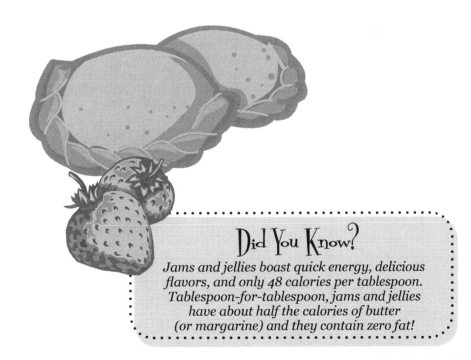

Did You Know?

Jams and jellies boast quick energy, delicious flavors, and only 48 calories per tablespoon. Tablespoon-for-tablespoon, jams and jellies have about half the calories of butter (or margarine) and they contain zero fat!

First Baseman's Never Fail Fudge

Prep: 10 minutes
Cook: 5 minutes
Makes: approximately 25 pieces

Ingredients:

3 cups semi-sweet chocolate chips

1 can (14 oz.) sweetened condensed milk

1 ½ tsp. vanilla extract

dash of salt

½ cup chopped nuts (optional)

Equipment:

Medium saucepan with lid

Wooden spoon

8" or 9" square glass baking pan

Measuring cups

Measuring spoons

Wax paper

"Don't be afraid to take advice. There's always something new to learn."
– Babe Ruth

Directions:

1. Prepare the glass pan by lining the bottom and sides with wax paper, allowing wax paper to extend at least an inch over the top and sides of the pan.

2. In a medium saucepan, combine the chocolate chips and sweetened condensed milk.

3. Cook on medium heat, stirring frequently until the chips are completely melted, about 5 minutes.

4. Remove the saucepan from the heat and add the vanilla extract, salt and nuts (optional).

5. Carefully pour mixture into the prepared pan.

6. Chill fudge until firm. Carefully remove and peel the wax paper from the fudge. Cut into 1 ½ inch squares.

Did You Know?

United States chocolate manufacturers use about 3.5 million pounds of whole milk every day to make chocolate. Sixty-five percent of American chocolate eaters prefer milk chocolate.

Umpire's Ultimate Banana Cream Pie

Prep: 15 minutes
Refrigerate: 2 hours
Makes: 8 servings

Ingredients:

1 package (5 oz.) instant vanilla pudding mix

2 cups low fat milk

½ cup sweetened condensed milk

1 package (8 oz.) low fat cream cheese, room temperature

1 container (12 oz.) whipped topping

4 to 6 medium bananas

2 tsp. lemon juice from 1 medium lemon

6 oz. low fat vanilla wafer cookies

Equipment:

Electric mixer

Small and medium mixing bowls

Measuring cups

Measuring spoons

Mixing spoon

Juicer

Serrated knife

Cutting board used for fruits and vegetables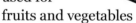

Table knife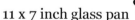

11 x 7 inch glass pan

Plastic wrap

"If you don't know where you're going, you might wind up somewhere else."
– Yogi Berra

Directions:

1. Using an electric mixer, mix together in a medium mixing bowl, the instant pudding mix with milk, sweetened condensed milk and cream cheese until smooth.

2. Fold in the whipped topping.

3. Peel the bananas. On a cutting board, slice each banana into ¼ inch slices.

4. Carefully cut the lemon in half and juice 2 teaspoons.

5. Gently toss the lemon juice with the sliced bananas in a small mixing bowl. This will help prevent the bananas from turning brown. Set aside.

6. To assemble the pie, first layer the wafer cookies touching next to each other on the bottom of the glass pan.

7. Next, layer half of the custard mixture, spreading evenly over the cookies.

8. Layer the bananas over the custard mixture.

9. Add remaining half of custard mixture, then put a final layer of the cookies on top.

10. Cover with plastic wrap and chill in the refrigerator for 2 hours or overnight before serving.

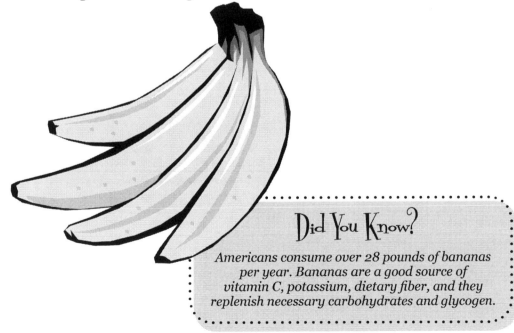

Did You Know?

Americans consume over 28 pounds of bananas per year. Bananas are a good source of vitamin C, potassium, dietary fiber, and they replenish necessary carbohydrates and glycogen.

Always a Winner Cherry Cheesecake Pies

Prep: 10 minutes
Bake: 15-20 minutes
Makes: 6 mini pies

Ingredients:

1 package graham cracker
mini pie crusts (6 to a pkg.)*

12 oz. cream cheese

¾ cup granulated sugar

2 large eggs

pinch of salt

1 can (14 oz.) cherry pie filling

Equipment:

Electric mixer

Small and medium mixing bowls

Measuring cups

Mixing spoon

Baking sheet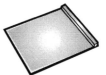

Can opener

Oven mitts

"Show class, have pride, and display character. If you do, winning takes care of itself."
– Paul "Bear" Bryant

Directions:

1. Preheat oven to 350°F.

2. In a medium mixing bowl, beat eggs together with an electric mixer until well blended.

3. Add the cream cheese, sugar and salt. Blend well until smooth.

4. Put the mini pie crusts on a baking sheet and fill them to the top with the cream cheese mixture.

5. Carefully put the baking sheet in the oven, and bake for 15 to 20 minutes, or until the pies are lightly golden on top.

6. Using oven mitts, carefully remove the pies from the oven and let them cool for an hour on the baking sheet.

7. Open the can of cherry pie filling with a can opener. Pour the pie filling into a small bowl and set aside.

8. When the pies are cool, spoon out two tablespoons of pie filling onto each mini cheesecake.

9. Refrigerate for at least 2 to 3 hours, or until ready to serve.

You may substitute 1 large 8 inch store bought graham cracker crust for the 6 mini pie crusts. Adjust baking time to 25 minutes, or until lightly golden on top.

Did You Know?

Cheesecake is believed to have originated in ancient Greece. Historians believe that cheesecake was served to the athletes during the first Olympic Games held in 776 B.C.

Quarterback Crunch Cookies

Prep: 10 minutes
Bake: 10-12 minutes
Makes: 4 dozen cookies

Ingredients:

1 cup shortening	1 cup quick cooking rolled oats
¾ cup granulated sugar	1 tsp. cream of tarter
¾ cup brown sugar	1 tsp. baking soda
1 cup vegetable oil	1 tsp. salt
2 large eggs	1 bag (12 oz.) chocolate chips
1 tsp. vanilla extract	1 cup crispy rice cereal
2 ¾ cups all-purpose flour	non-stick cooking spray

Equipment:

Electric mixer

Large mixing bowl

Measuring cups

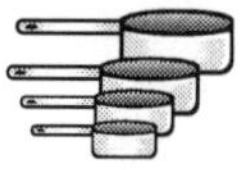

Measuring spoons

Large mixing spoon

Baking sheet(s)

Small spatula

Oven mitts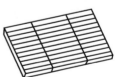

Wire cooling rack

"Before you can win, you have to believe you are worthy."
– Mike Ditka

Directions:

1. Preheat oven to 350°F.

2. Using an electric mixer on low speed, combine the shortening, sugars, vegetable oil, eggs and vanilla. Beat for about 2 minutes, or until well blended.

3. Add flour, oatmeal, cream of tarter, baking soda and salt. Mix until just combined.

4. Carefully stir in chocolate chips and crispy rice cereal.

5. Prepare the baking sheet(s) by spraying the bottom with non-stick cooking spray.

6. Drop dough by rounded tablespoonfuls onto the baking sheet.

7. Bake for 10-12 minutes, or until cookies are light brown.

8. Using oven mitts, carefully remove the baking sheet from the oven.

9. Let the cookies set for a few minutes before transferring them to a wire cooling rack to finish cooling.

Did You Know?

The first cookies were created by accident. Bakers used a small amount of cake batter to test their oven temperature before baking a large cake.

Kyle's Touchdown Toffee Bars

Prep: 10 minutes
Bake: 5-7 minutes
Refrigerate: 30 minutes
Makes: 24 pieces

Ingredients:

12 graham crackers (approximately), broken in quarters

1 cup firmly packed brown sugar

1 cup butter (do not substitute)

1 cup semi-sweet chocolate chips

½ cup toffee bits

non-stick cooking spray

Equipment:

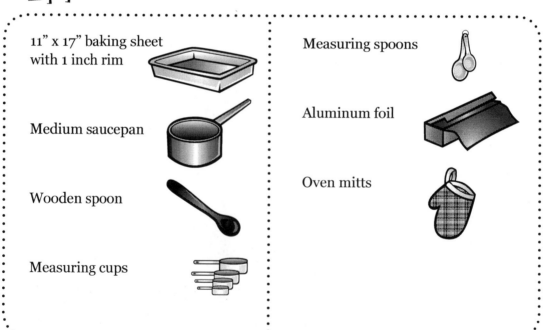

11" x 17" baking sheet with 1 inch rim

Medium saucepan

Wooden spoon

Measuring cups

Measuring spoons

Aluminum foil

Oven mitts

"Do right. Do your best. Treat others as you want to be treated."
– Lou Holtz

Directions:

1. Preheat oven to 400°F.

2. Line the baking sheet or jelly roll pan with foil. Spray with non-stick cooking spray.

3. Arrange the graham crackers so that they are touching next to each other. The entire pan must be covered. You may have to break them to make them fit.

4. In a medium saucepan, combine the brown sugar and butter. Stir constantly until boiling, about 2 minutes.

5. Pour mixture over graham crackers.

6. Put the pan in the oven and bake for 2 minutes.

7. Using oven mitts, carefully remove the pan from the oven and immediately sprinkle the top with chocolate chips.

8. Using oven mitts again, return the pan to the oven for 2 minutes more, until chips are melted.

9. Continue to use the oven mitts and carefully remove the pan from the oven and sprinkle with toffee bits.

10. Chill in the freezer or refrigerator for at least 30 minutes or until the chocolate is set.

11. Break into pieces, and store covered in the refrigerator or freezer.

Fun Trivia

Which do you like better: toffee or caramel? Actually, they are basically the same thing; melted butter and sugar. Toffee is cooked at a higher temperature which makes it crunchy, and caramel is cooked at a lower temperature keeping it soft and chewy. I always make these toffee bars during the holidays and bring in a box for my teacher. Yes, a little sweet bribe never hurt anyone. ;-)

Hockey Team's Best Lemon Bars

Prep: 10 minutes
Bake: 30 minutes
Makes: 16 servings

Ingredients:

1 package lemon cake mix

½ cup vegetable oil

2 large eggs

1 package (8 oz.) cream cheese

1/3 cup granulated sugar

1 Tbs. lemon juice

1 Tbs. all-purpose flour

1 tsp. baking powder

non-stick cooking spray

Equipment:

Medium and small mixing bowl

Measuring cups

Measuring spoons

Whisk

Wooden spoon

8" or 9" glass square baking pan

Serrated knife

Small spatula

Oven mitts

"A good hockey player plays where the puck is. A great hockey player plays where the puck is going to be."
– Wayne Gretzky

Directions:

1. Preheat oven to 350°F.

2. Prepare the baking dish by spraying the bottom and sides with non-stick cooking spray.

3. In a medium mixing bowl, combine the cake mix, vegetable oil and 1 egg. Set aside 1 cup of this dough mixture for topping.

4. Pat the rest of the dough mixture onto bottom of the baking pan and bake for 10 to 15 minutes, or until the crust is lightly golden.

5. In a small mixing bowl, combine 1 egg, cream cheese, sugar, lemon juice, flour and baking powder. Beat well until thoroughly mixed.

6. After 10 to 15 minutes of baking, carefully remove the pan from the oven using oven mitts. Pour cream cheese mixture over the baked crust.

7. Drop by teaspoonfuls, the remaining cake dough mixture onto the cream cheese mixture. Use oven mitts again, and return pan to the oven for 10 minutes longer, or until lightly golden on top.

8. Remove pan from the oven, continuing to use the oven mitts.

9. Cool the bars completely before cutting with a serrated knife.

Did You Know?

The origins of lemon bars appear to lie in the 1930's, when bakers started making more cookies in large sheet pans. Lemon bars appear to have hit the popular imagination in the 1960's, although some variations may have been made before this period.

In the Bullpen Double Chocolate Brownies

Prep: 10 minutes
Bake: 25 minutes
Makes: 9 servings

Ingredients:

¾ cup butter

1 cup granulated sugar

1 tsp. vanilla extract

3 large eggs

¾ cup all-purpose flour

½ cup unsweetened cocoa powder

½ tsp. baking powder

½ tsp. salt

1 cup chocolate chips

non-stick cooking spray

Equipment:

8" or 9" square glass baking pan

Medium microwave safe mixing bowl

Measuring cups

Measuring spoons

Mixing spoon

Oven mitts

*"Good, better, best. Never let it rest. Until your good
is better and your better is best."*
– Unknown

Directions:

1 Preheat oven to 350°F.

2 In a microwave safe mixing bowl, melt the butter in the microwave oven.

3 Carefully remove the bowl from the oven. Let the butter cool slightly.

4 Add the sugar, vanilla extract and eggs. Beat for 1 minute.

5 Add flour, unsweetened cocoa powder, baking powder, salt and chocolate chips. Mix until well blended. Batter will be very stiff.

6 Prepare the baking pan by spraying the bottom and sides with non-stick cooking spray.

7 Pour batter in the pan. Bake for 25 minutes or when a toothpick inserted 1 inch from the side of the brownie pan comes out clean.

8 Using oven mitts, carefully remove brownies from the oven.

9 Let the brownies set a few minutes before cutting.

Did You Know?

Chocolate brownies didn't become widely popular until the 1920's, when chocolate became more readily available.

All American Apple Soda

Ingredients:

1 can (12 oz.) unsweetened frozen apple juice concentrate, thawed

4 cups of any clear carbonated soda, or club soda

Equipment:

Large pitcher

Liquid measuring cup

Wooden spoon

Directions:

1 Pour the concentrated apple juice and soda in a large pitcher.

2 Stir together. Pour in 6 individual glasses with ice.

"Never let the fear of striking out get in your way."
– Babe Ruth

Just for Fun!

Puzzles and More

Scan Me!

Want the Answers?

Test your sports knowledge on the next few pages.
Find all the solutions to the puzzles by
scanning the QR Code. No cheating!

Baseball Crossword

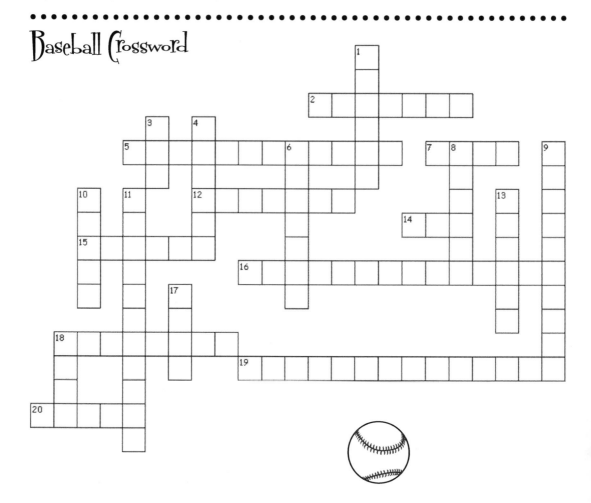

Across

2. One player bunts, the other steals home

5. A fly ball that is caught, but scores a run (2 words)

7. An infield hit where the hitter doesn't fully swing the bat

12. Sticky substance used for better grip (2 words)

14. Run batted in

15. Not a ball

16. Younger of the two leagues (2 words)

18. The Great Bambino (2 words)

19. This league was found in the 1870's (2 words)

20. The tool used by players in the field

Down

1. Two base hit

3. Wooden stick

4. Three base hit

6. Player who teams up with pitcher on every play

8. The person behind the catcher

9. Area over the plate between the knee and torso (2 words)

10. Three white bags on the field

11. The best teams from each league playing for the championship (2 words)

13. Base hit

17. Ball hit out of play

18. Not a strike; the other half of base _____

Baseball Word Search

Find the basketball words below in the word search grid. The words can be forwards or backwards, vertical, horizontal, or diagonal. Circle each letter separately, but keep in mind that the letters may be used in more than one word. When the word search puzzle is complete, read the remaining letters left to right and top to bottom, to learn an interesting baseball fact.

```
H  I  N  N  I  N  G  S  B  T  R  I  P  L  E
O  O  S  T  O  N  S  A  C  R  I  F  I  C  E
M  B  E  A  T  P  I  U  T  L  A  E  T  S  S
E  S  A  B  T  S  R  I  F  T  S  B  C  U  T
R  O  R  R  E  V  R  G  C  A  T  C  H  E  R
U  H  E  I  E  S  L  I  D  I  N  G  E  N  I
N  T  S  B  H  E  F  I  D  R  U  L  R  M  K
S  B  A  S  E  H  I  T  L  T  B  L  D  A  E
E  L  B  W  R  E  D  L  E  I  F  A  I  L  R
L  O  D  R  L  R  T  H  I  R  D  B  A  S  E
B  D  N  S  E  I  R  I  F  E  U  F  M  D  T
U  H  O  M  E  P  L  A  T  E  G  O  O  N  T
O  S  C  A  P  M  B  O  U  T  O  U  N  A  A
D  Y  E  F  I  U  V  E  O  T  U  L  D  R  B
O  T  S  T  A  D  I  U  M  H  T  R  E  G  E
```

BALL	ERROR	PITCHER
BASE HIT	FIELDER	SACRIFICE
BATTER	FIRST BASE	SECOND BASE
BUNT	FOUL	SLIDING
CAP	GRAND SLAM	STADIUM
CATCHER	HOME PLATE	STEAL
CURVE BALL	HOME RUN	STRIKE
DIAMOND	INNINGS	THIRD BASE
DOUBLE	OUT	TRIPLE
DUGOUT	OUTFIELD	UMPIRE

Basketball Crossword

Across

2. Towering player in the middle
4. Taking the ball from a player
5. 24 seconds counter (2 words)
7. The hoop
9. Not a layup, dunk, or three pointer
10. Michael Jordan's highlight shot (2 words)
11. Shot usually played off the backboard
14. Both hands bounce (2 words)
16. Backboard
17. Floor general (2 words)

Down

1. Sitting on the pine
2. Line where foul shot is taken (2 words)
3. Attached to the rim
4. Kobe Bryant's position (2 words)
6. The paint
8. Begins the game
12. Turn around flip shot over the shoulder
13. Grabbing a missed shot
15. Deflecting a shot in the air
18. Three point line

Basketball Word Search

Find the basketball words below in the word search grid. The words can be forwards or backwards, vertical, horizontal, or diagonal. Circle each letter separately, but keep in mind that the letters may be used in more than one word. When the word search puzzle is complete, read the remaining letters left to right and top to bottom, to learn an interesting basketball fact.

```
J J A B F M E K S B N A I F S
U M I O A T H C L T O V I P W
M A R X S S W O R H T E E R F
P T E O T H C L E C L A Y U P
B A T U B K N C A D D I A N A
A B N T R Y W T G H O F D T L
L A E P E R S O N A L F O U L
L C C K A A A H I T N O U R E
V K E H K L M S E O F P B N Y
N B T P A S S K K O O I L O O
C O U R T R S G N H R T E V O
E A D B A A G A U S W S T E P
D R I B B L E E D A A K E R E
T D N L U O F T N A R G A L F
J U M P S H O T B A D D M L L
```

ALLEY-OOP	**DUNK**	**LAY-UP**
BACKBOARD	**FAST BREAK**	**NBA**
BASKET	**FIELD GOAL**	**PASS**
BLOCK	**FLAGRANT FOUL**	**PERSONAL FOUL**
BOX OUT	**FORWARD**	**PIVOT**
CENTER	**FREE THROW**	**SHOOT**
CHARGE	**GUARD**	**SHOT CLOCK**
COURT	**JUMP BALL**	**TEAM**
DOUBLE TEAM	**JUMP SHOT**	**TIP-OFF**
DRIBBLE	**KEY**	**TURNOVER**

Football Crossword

Down

1. The biggest game of the year (2 words)
2. Touchdown area (2 words)
3. One point kick
4. Players trying to sack the quarterback
7. Poles the ball is kicked between
8. First down distance (2 words)
9. Technique of taking a player to the ground
10. Pigskin
12. The cage in front of the helmet (2 words)
14. Tackling the quarterback behind the line of scrimmage

Across

5. Protective head covering
6. First year in the league
10. Three points (2 words)
11. The AFC and NFC combined
13. Big shoulders
15. Defensive players covering wide receivers
16. Out of bounds

Football Word Search

Find the basketball words below in the word search grid. The words can be forwards or backwards, vertical, horizontal, or diagonal. Circle each letter separately, but keep in mind that the letters may be used in more than one word. When the word search puzzle is complete, read the remaining letters left to right and top to bottom, to learn an interesting football fact.

```
A  K  W  Q  U  K  C  A  B  F  L  A  H  A  R
T  L  I  N  E  B  A  C  K  E  R  E  R  B  T
A  C  D  C  K  R  E  C  E  I  U  V  E  K  I
S  T  E  E  K  C  A  B  R  E  N  R  O  C  G
H  E  R  S  L  E  N  A  M  E  N  I  L  A  H
N  A  E  P  T  K  R  K  H  K  I  E  N  B  T
S  T  C  O  S  D  C  C  C  E  N  T  E  R  E
R  S  E  R  E  N  S  A  I  T  G  T  O  E  N
E  A  I  R  E  E  B  B  T  U  B  N  F  T  D
V  N  V  I  N  T  G  L  B  A  A  C  L  R  K
I  T  E  H  O  I  N  L  R  O  C  W  A  A  S
E  T  R  L  O  L  A  U  R  E  K  U  N  U  C
C  E  S  I  V  P  E  F  P  R  G  O  K  Q  R
E  R  U  N  S  S  A  F  E  T  Y  W  E  I  T
R  E  P  P  A  N  S  G  N  O  L  H  R  I  T
```

CENTER	PUNTER
CORNERBACK	QUARTERBACK
FLANKER	RECEIVERS
FULLBACK	RUNNING BACK
GUARD	SAFETY
HALFBACK	SLOTBACK
KICKER	SPLIT END
LINEBACKER	TACKLE
LINEMAN	TIGHT END
LONG SNAPPER	WIDE RECEIVER

Hockey Crossword

Across

2. This is what you wear on your feet for this sport.

7. A _____ is a hard, black rubber disc used to score goals.

8. When a hockey player scores three goals in one game.

9. This penalty is when a player trips an opposing player with their stick, or uses their skate against the other skate.

11. Free to skate and shoot.

Down

1. A _____ in ice hockey is worth one point.

3. When a player swings his stick back and then forward to strike the puck with maximum force toward the goal.

4. Hockey players use this piece of equipment to hit a hockey puck with.

5. What player defends the net in ice hockey?

6. The place where you play ice hockey.

10. What surface is professional hockey played?

12. This shot uses arm muscles to propel a puck forward from the concave side of the stick.

Hockey Word Search

Find the basketball words below in the word search grid. The words can be forwards or backwards, vertical, horizontal, or diagonal. Circle each letter separately, but keep in mind that the letters may be used in more than one word. When the word search puzzle is complete, read the remaining letters left to right and top to bottom, to learn an interesting hockey fact.

```
S L A S H I N G N I D L O H F
A N E R A O L H N L Y M P S A
I C E N T E R G N I K C E H C
C T H Y T L A N E P P T O C E
P O W E R P L A Y K A P E Y O
W H D N I E B U T K E U I D F
R S H O C K E Y S T I C K R F
I P O Z K I N A W I N Y T O T
S A O L F O R W A R D E T F D
T L K A E T E A M R O L E F E
S S I R F T F K N I N N M S F
H E N T T R E A E G O A L I E
O E G U E O R E N T W T E D N
T H R E E P E R I O D S H E S
E N T N Y S E B L U E L I N E
```

ARENA	HELMET	REFEREE
BLUE LINE	HOCKEY STICK	SKATES
BREAKAWAY	HOLDING	SLAPSHOT
CENTER	HOOKING	SLASHING
CHECKING	NET	SPORT
DEFENSE	NEUTRAL ZONE	STANLEY CUP
FACE-OFF	NHL	TEAM
FORWARD	OFFSIDE	THREE PERIODS
GOALIE	PENALTY	TRIPPING
HAT TRICK	POWER PLAY	WRIST SHOT

Across

4. The last one who can stop your opponent from scoring.

6. An illegal use of arms or hands.

7. If you mark someone, you are _____.

9. Soccer players use their _____ to control the ball.

10. A penalty kick is also knows as a _____ kick.

11. A serious caution is know as a _____ card.

Down

1. Spanish for soccer.

2. The _____ Cup is held every four years.

3. The shoes that soccer players wear.

5. When tossing the ball inbounds, be sure you don't go over the _____.

6. Goalies can use their _____ only inside the big box around the goal.

8. Defenders should try to kick the ball to the _____ and not the middle.

Soccer Word Search

Find the basketball words below in the word search grid. The words can be forwards or backwards, vertical, horizontal, or diagonal. Circle each letter separately, but keep in mind that the letters may be used in more than one word. When the word search puzzle is complete, read the remaining letters left to right and top to bottom, to learn an interesting soccer fact.

```
G  N  I  K  C  I  K  S  O  C  C  E  R  I  S
C  I  A  L  L  H  E  D  F  O  O  C  T  B  A
T  N  E  V  E  C  I  P  M  Y  L  O  L  R  R
L  E  I  A  N  M  O  S  S  T  P  R  A  E  R
T  T  D  D  S  O  S  G  F  T  D  N  F  D  H
E  Y  W  D  R  A  C  W  O  L  L  E  Y  C  O
R  M  L  F  P  I  D  A  E  A  R  R  N  A  D
I  I  S  O  S  T  B  I  H  E  L  K  F  R  P
O  N  D  O  U  G  F  B  E  H  T  I  T  D  U
O  U  A  T  B  E  T  H  L  E  F  C  E  M  C
O  T  P  B  S  T  P  O  P  E  U  K  L  A  D
P  E  N  A  L  T  Y  K  I  C  K  R  S  P  L
O  S  I  L  R  T  I  N  G  N  I  N  N  U  R
T  H  H  L  L  A  B  D  N  A  H  E  W  H  O
O  L  S  T  A  E  L  C  E  W  O  R  L  D  W
```

CLEATS	NINETY MINUTES
CORNER KICK	OLYMPIC EVENT
DRIBBLE	PASS
FIELD	PENALTY KICK
FIFA	RED CARD
FOOTBALL	REFEREE
GOALIE	RUNNING
HAND BALL	SHIN PADS
HEAD	WORLD CUP
KICKING	YELLOW CARD

My Recipe Journal

Recipe: On the Mound Easy Cheesy Mac and Cheese　　**Date:** June 15, 2015

Tasty Rating: 😕 😐 🙂 😁

Difficulty Rating: ◐ ▣ ◈ ◈◈

Overall Rating: 👎 👉 👍 👍👍

Notes: I made this recipe for my whole family, even though Dad thought it was all for him since it was close to Father's Day. He sure ate a lot! I added a few crumbled corn chips on top of each serving for an extra crunch. Yum! Mom said it was a perfectly complete meal with the On Deck Ranch Salad that she and I prepared together.

Recipe: _____　　**Date:** _____

Tasty Rating: 😕 😐 🙂 😁

Difficulty Rating: ◐ ▣ ◈ ◈◈

Overall Rating: 👎 👉 👍 👍👍

Notes: _____

_____

_____

Legend

Tasty Rating:	Difficulty Rating:
😕 I'm glad I tried it, but not exactly my thing	◐ Pretty easy (like level 1 on my video game)
😐 I'll eat it again, but it's not my favorite	▣ Some easy parts, some hard parts (kind of like my math tests)
🙂 Satisfying and delicious	◈ Challenging, but fun (greater the effort, greater the reward)
😁 **Yum!** I could eat this every day	◈◈ A little tough, but practice (and an adult helper) makes perfect

Recipe: **Date:**

Tasty Rating: 😕 😐 🙂 😁

Difficulty Rating:

Overall Rating:

Notes: _____
_____
_____
_____

Recipe: **Date:**

Tasty Rating: 😕 😐 🙂 😁

Difficulty Rating:

Overall Rating:

Notes: _____
_____
_____
_____

Recipe: **Date:**

Tasty Rating: 😕 😐 🙂 😁

Difficulty Rating:

Overall Rating:

Notes: _____
_____
_____
_____

Recipe: _____ **Date:** _____

Tasty Rating: 😕 😐 🙂 😁

Difficulty Rating:

Overall Rating:

Notes: _____
_____
_____
_____

Recipe: _____ **Date:** _____

Tasty Rating: 😕 😐 🙂 😁

Difficulty Rating:

Overall Rating:

Notes: _____
_____
_____
_____

Recipe: _____ **Date:** _____

Tasty Rating: 😕 😐 🙂 😁

Difficulty Rating:

Overall Rating:

Notes: _____
_____
_____

Recipe: _____   **Date:** _____

Tasty Rating: 😕   😐   🙂   😁

Difficulty Rating: ◯   ▢   ◇   ◇◇

Overall Rating: 👎   👈   👍   👍👍

Notes: _____
_____
_____
_____

Recipe: _____   **Date:** _____

Tasty Rating: 😕   😐   🙂   😁

Difficulty Rating: ◯   ▢   ◇   ◇◇

Overall Rating: 👎   👈   👍   👍👍

Notes: _____
_____
_____
_____

Recipe: _____   **Date:** _____

Tasty Rating: 😕   😐   🙂   😁

Difficulty Rating: ◯   ▢   ◇   ◇◇

Overall Rating: 👎   👈   👍   👍👍

Notes: _____
_____
_____
_____

Recipe: _____ **Date:** _____

Tasty Rating: 🙁 😐 🙂 😁

Difficulty Rating: ⬭ ▢ ◆ ◆◆

Overall Rating: 👎 👉 👍 👍👍

Notes: _____
_____
_____
_____

Recipe: _____ **Date:** _____

Tasty Rating: 🙁 😐 🙂 😁

Difficulty Rating: ⬭ ▢ ◆ ◆◆

Overall Rating: 👎 👉 👍 👍👍

Notes: _____
_____
_____
_____

Recipe: _____ **Date:** _____

Tasty Rating: 🙁 😐 🙂 😁

Difficulty Rating: ⬭ ▢ ◆ ◆◆

Overall Rating: 👎 👉 👍 👍👍

Notes: _____
_____
_____
_____

Recipe: **Date:**

Tasty Rating:

Difficulty Rating:

Overall Rating:

Notes: _____

_____

_____

_____

Recipe: **Date:**

Tasty Rating:

Difficulty Rating:

Overall Rating:

Notes: _____

_____

_____

_____

Recipe: **Date:**

Tasty Rating:

Difficulty Rating:

Overall Rating:

Notes: _____

_____

_____

_____

Recipe Index

About the Author

Kelly Lambrakis is an editor, writer and a health food enthusiast. She is a widow and has three young boys, living in Southern California. She has always loved spending time in the kitchen. Her mother taught her how to cook at a very young age. As a little girl, they loved making favorite recipes together, including homemade treats for family and friends to enjoy. Years later, she continued that tradition, making it a priority to include her children in the kitchen, like her mother did, in hopes that her boys would enjoy cooking too.

Kelly is the author of the popular **Boys Can Cook Too!** and the **Cooking with Kids** series of cookbooks. With her passion for healthy eating, she believes that it's not difficult or time consuming to eat clean, healthy foods, and to teach our children to do the same. Her series of **Cooking with Kids interactive cookbooks** are sold in Paperback and in Kindle format in hopes that many adults and children will easily access quick and healthy recipes that anyone can make. Her most recent cookbooks range from healthy quick snacks, allergy sensitive recipes, including easy soups, lunchbox favorites, and 5 ingredient healthy meals that the whole family can enjoy, even during busy, active schedules.

More Cooking with Kid's Books

Cooking with Kids - Healthy Snacks
Quick and Healthy Recipes to make with Kids in 10 minutes or less!

Cooking with Kids - Just 5 Ingredients
Healthy Recipes for Busy Families on the Go!

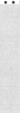

Cooking with Kids - Allergy Free
Favorite Whole Food Recipes for Allergy Friendly and Low Sugar Cooking!

Cooking with Kids - Cookies and More!
Sweet Treats and Healthy Options for Kids that love to Bake!

Fundraising Opportunities

Scan Me!

We Love to Help!

Are you interested in raising money to help

a worthy cause in your community?

We support schools, youth groups and clubs,

as well as charitable non-profits.

Visit

www.CookingWithKids4YourHealth.com

to learn more!

Rave Reviews

"I was really pleased to see a book that not only encourages boys to cook but makes it "cool". My boys, ages 7 and 12, were both very eager to read the book and pick out recipes that appealed to them. The sports angle really attracted them. What a wonderful way to spend quality time with your boys. I can't wait to start giving them as gifts to other families with sports lovin' boys."

- Mom of 2 boys, Seattle, WA

"I got this book for my birthday and I really love it. The recipes are very easy and fun to make. I also like reading the sports quotes and doing the puzzles in the back of the book. Can't wait for the next book!"

- Jordan, Fort Lauderdale, FL

"What a great idea - to provide boys with a working knowledge of cooking and baking. Wish it would have been around when I was growing up. As my son's coach, we love reading the sports quotes together. Plus the recipes are easy, to the point, and most importantly, delicious for the whole team to enjoy."

- John Y., Reading, PA

"My Uncle got this book for me and I've been making a ton of food ever since. My favorite recipes so far are the Pumpkin Chili and Quarterback Crunch Cookies. Thanks so much for making a cookbook for boys! It's awesome!"

- Daniel, Newport Beach, CA

"As the mom of a sports lovin' boy myself, I look for opportunities to spend time with him off the field. This book is an invitation for my son to join me in the kitchen, be creative, and share my passion of cooking for my family and friends. What a great gift for that sporty boy who has every piece of equipment and pack of baseball cards out there!"

- Tami, Omaha, NE

Made in the USA
Middletown, DE
21 February 2019